Miss Conduct's
Mind Over Manners

Miss Conduct's

MIND OVER MANNERS

Master the Slippery Rules
of Modern
Ethics and Etiquette

❖

ROBIN ABRAHAMS

Times Books
Henry Holt and Company · New York

Times Books
Henry Holt and Company, LLC
Publishers since 1866
175 Fifth Avenue
New York, New York 10010
www.henryholt.com

Henry Holt® is a registered trademark of
Henry Holt and Company, LLC.

Library of Congress Cataloging-in-Publication Data

Abrahams, Robin.
Miss Conduct's mind over manners : master the slippery rules of modern
ethics and etiquette / Robin Abrahams.—1st ed.
    p.   cm.
Includes bibliographical references and index.
ISBN-13: 978-0-8050-8877-9
ISBN-10: 0-8050-8877-6
1. Etiquette.   I. Title.
BJ1853.A27 2009
395—dc22   2008049090

Henry Holt books are available for special promotions
and premiums. For details contact: Director, Special Markets.

First Edition 2009
Designed by Victoria Hartman

Printed in the United States of America

P1

To my mother and my father,
and to my readers

Contents

Miss Conduct's
Mind Over Manners

Introduction

WELCOME TO THE REAL WORLD
OF ETIQUETTE

"People come at life from different places, they
understand the world in different ways, they strive for
different ends. This is a fact that has proved amazingly
hard to live with."

—Louis Menand, *The Metaphysical Club*

Admit it: you're not sure what the rules are anymore.

Oh, not the rules about not doing unto others as that which
would be hateful unto you, or loving thy neighbor as thyself.
You know the *big* rules. And all the little ones about which fork
to use when and the proper order of a wedding processional?
Maybe you even know those, or at least you have a dusty book
in which you can look them up as necessary.

No, nowadays, the problems that flummox people are the
dilemmas that live in the gray area between ethics (the big rules)
and protocol (the small ones), and reflect the modern explosion
of social complexity. Problems like:

- Is it polite to say "Bless you" to a sneezing atheist?
- Is there a good way to request "No Barbies or Disney
princesses, please" for a four-year-old's birthday party?

- What, if anything, should be said to an otherwise health-conscious friend who is tanning himself into jerky?
- Can a group of women properly be addressed as "you guys"?

And my personal favorite—

- What's a nice vegetarian girl to do if Gypsies give her bread smeared with lard?

The first thing you should understand: it's not just you who is confused. (You can calm down about that.) The second thing: there are no *rules* yet devised for these slippery questions—but there are principles of conduct that will gracefully guide your way through the world. Seductively simple as rules are, they're no longer adequate for the modern world.

In the three generations since Emily Post debuted her bible of propriety, unprecedented diversity has marked our lives—not just diversity of race, ethnicity, and religion, but of *priorities, values*, and *experiences*. Every culture has its ideologies, its traditions, its folklore—about what we can and cannot eat; how to share and display our material resources; how to make sense of the world around us and create rituals for the transitions of our lives; how men and women should interact; and how to treat children, the sick and disabled, and domestic animals. Food, money, religion, children, sex and relationships, health, and pets—these are the topics people ask "Miss Conduct" about, and so these are the chapters of my book. Figuring out the answers to those questions is a large part of what culture is *for*.

In twenty-first-century America, finding these answers is exceedingly complicated. People who choose not to have children maintain that their decision is as positive—and their time as valuable—as that of parents. Vegetarians and people who follow religious or health-related dietary rules are less willing to "eat a little just to be polite." And let's not even get into the whole business of who wants to be cheered with a "Merry Christmas" and who does not (at least not until chapter 3, anyway). Throughout history, new technology—from the printing press to the BlackBerry—and new ideas—from Manifest Destiny to multiculturalism—have driven changes in social behavior. But people don't all react to change in a coordinated fashion, like a school of fish suddenly veering away from a shark. Everyone processes change at different rates. This means that for any situation there are probably quite a few versions of "correct" behavior to choose from—and quite a few people willing to say that you didn't choose the "right" one.

Food, money, religion, children, sex and relationships, health, and pets—there's a reason these are the things people wonder about; this stuff has been important to us humans for a very, very long time. Without all those things, and our ability to think about them, we wouldn't even *be* human. So in each chapter, I start by explaining a bit about the evolutionary roots of each issue and then try to describe, as best I can, the different cultural values bumping together in the twenty-first century. I offer advice on how to live with your own values and how to live with those who have chosen different ones.

It's worth mentioning that, for all the talk of "culture war" and "red" and "blue" states, I almost never get questions that are directly political in nature.* Instead, the real-world power struggles of social engagement play out in office kitchenettes, where

---

* Every once in a while I receive a question along the lines of "How do I stop my left-wing/right-wing sister from forwarding me e-mails she knows will raise my blood pressure?" but that's about it.

Indian immigrants microwave homemade fish curries to the discomfort of their American-born colleagues; at coffee-shop counters, where women just returning from maternity leave casually reveal their salaries and breast-pumping routines to their horrified friends; in subway cars, where young women wonder if they can offer elderly men their seats without making them feel less manly; and in college dorm rooms, where offhand references to vacation homes and cleaning ladies make sons of blue-collar families feel left out. Perhaps every generation since time began has felt that they are living in an era of unprecedented change and upheaval—and, hey, perhaps they were right. But for us, here and now, there needs to be some guidance in how to negotiate our changing times—from women's progress and immigrant arrivals (and the backlashes to them, and the backlashes to the backlashes) to the disappearance of the "company man" and the creation of an insecure "free-agent nation."

As social change continues to accelerate, following the rules of manners is no longer enough—we need *mind*. We need to *think*. Rules may have worked in the days when everyone agreed on the same set of priorities: that decent people never talk about money or sex, that children should be seen and not heard, and that vegetarians or observant Jews should simply shut up about their weird practices and eat the hamburger-macaroni-and-cheese casserole in front of them gratefully, because there were children starving (quietly!) in China. Perhaps life was never quite as neat and predictable as all *that*, but it was a good deal more like that once upon a time than it is now. I'm not by any means saying that the traditional rules of etiquette should be tossed by the wayside. I'll stand up for a thank-you note every time. Rather, I'm saying that it's more important to look at the underlying purpose for the old rules and find useful principles for living life graciously today.

The Rudeness Epidemic

Most Americans think we're experiencing an epidemic of rudeness. In a 2005 poll conducted by Ipsos Public Affairs, 69 percent of respondents said that people—*other* people, of course, and mostly younger people—had gotten ruder over the past twenty to thirty years. Is the perception true? Who knows? The question of whether people really are ruder today than in some mythical "yesterday" is hardly the kind of question that can be measured scientifically. Interestingly, the poll was released just a few days before the death of the great civil rights leader Rosa Parks. I could not help but wonder how Parks, who grew up in an era when it was perfectly polite to address a black man as "boy" and expect him to ride in the back of the bus, would have felt about today's standards of politeness compared to yesterday's.

Another survey, ominously titled "Aggravating Circumstances: A Status Report on Rudeness in America" and taken in 2002, found an even higher proportion of Americans—79 percent—agreeing that "lack of respect and courtesy is a serious problem in our society." Despite the overwhelming agreement on this issue, the sample was evenly split as to whether the perceived decline in civility was caused by many people or an uncouth yet memorable few. Forty-one percent of respondents, in a surprising show of honesty, admitted to violating their own codes of civility. The reality of the situation can never be measured objectively, but if almost everyone believes that civilization is in decline, then clearly there is a problem that needs to be addressed. Belief is as important as reality.

So did we all just wake up one day in the 1970s and turn into schmucks? I don't think so. Based on societal trends, I believe that the perception of a rudeness epidemic comes from two main, interrelated sources: 1) forces that make it difficult to prioritize politeness, and 2) the increased complication of being polite, even when you want to be.

Why does politeness fall off the radar screen so easily? In the "Aggravating Circumstances" study, nearly half the people surveyed believed that a major cause of rudeness is the fact that "life is so hectic and people are so busy and pressed for time that they forget to be polite." Even more—61 percent—said that they themselves had been too busy to be polite. Writing thank-you notes, paying hospital visits, organizing dinner parties, buying birthday presents—these things take time. Even smaller everyday courtesies require emotional and intellectual energy. There's a reason we call it "thoughtfulness": being actively kind to people requires *thought*. And when you're stressed out and busy, you might not have the bandwidth to be thoughtful of others.

Research on whether people are really working more than they did twenty-five years ago is varied. Some scholars find that we are, others that we're not. But what no one can dispute is that people certainly believe that they're working more. E-mail, cell phones, and BlackBerrys have made it possible to be on call 24/7; even when you're not working, your time doesn't feel entirely private. The boundaries between work and home have blurred.

Home itself is no refuge at that. Housewives of the 1950s played bridge while their kids biked around the suburbs. The ideology of parenthood a generation ago was to let kids be kids, with parents providing discipline and security and a fair amount of benign neglect. Remember the phrase "He's growing like a weed"? Today's kids don't grow like weeds, they grow like hothouse orchids. Parents are expected to be deeply involved in their children's lives, playing with them, coaching them, helping them with schoolwork, driving them to soccer practice. Being a mother used to be a relationship; now it's a job.

Wherever you look you see the bar rising in a similar fashion. Retirement planning used to mean finding a secure job with a pension; now it requires monitoring your investments and meeting with a financial planner every quarter. "Taking care of yourself" used to mean an annual checkup and some moisturizer at night; now it means triweekly gym visits, tooth whitening, calorie counting, sunblocking, cholesterol managing, and meditating. Entertaining friends used to require little more than a deck of cards and a six-pack; Martha Stewart put an end to that. Everywhere, there is pressure to do more, do better, and look fantastic and youthful while you're doing it. When our time, energy, and budgets are sapped by such demands, we quickly become too tired and cranky and stressed to be polite.

It's no wonder we don't have the energy to write thank-you notes. And our rapidly complexifying society doesn't make it any easier.

Diversity and Its Discontents

We all know we ought to celebrate diversity or at least tolerate it—the implication being that if we don't, we're a bunch of nasty, narrow-minded nativists. If only coping well with diversity could be achieved by looking into one's heart and finding love for one's neighbor! Still not easy, perhaps, but simple. But tolerance for diversity is more than a character trait. It's real, hard work, and it goes against our nature.

We evolved as tribal creatures, attached to our own, suspicious of the other. From an evolutionary point of view, fear of difference isn't a bug, it's a feature—we evolved to be suspicious of those we don't know, those who look or act different, because such people may have bad intent toward us or be carrying diseases to which we are not immune. Because of our evolutionary heritage, people tend to react to diversity in predictable ways. Increased demographic diversity and social change (which nearly always go hand in hand) frequently lead to a loss in the sense of community, an increased desire to hunker down with our own kind, and the decay of common cultural touchstones—all of which decrease our motivation to be polite.

Almost all advanced countries, including the United States, have seen tremendous growth in ethnic diversity in the past twenty years. According to a disturbing study by the sociologist Robert Putnam, author of *Bowling Alone: The Collapse and Revival of American Community,* increased ethnic and racial diversity has a negative effect on people's sociability. People don't become prejudiced against "the other" as you might expect; instead they withdraw from everyone, even people in their own demographic group. In ethnically or racially diverse neighborhoods, people have less confidence in local leadership and media; have less belief that they can influence their communities; are less likely to register to vote; are less trusting of their neighbors' ability to cooperate to solve community problems; are less likely to work on or give to a community project or a charity; have fewer close friends; report less happiness and satisfaction with their lives; and spend more time watching television. Increasing diversity alienates us from our neighborhoods.

At the same time, American culture is fragmenting into smaller and smaller niches of distinct values, priorities, and experiences. This trend is documented in *The Big Sort: Why the*

Clustering of Like-Minded America Is Tearing Us Apart, a remarkable book by Bill Bishop. Since the 1970s—and accelerating through the 1990s—people have been moving to neighborhoods that reflect their lifestyle preferences and values. If I told you my zip code, you could probably guess pretty accurately for whom I voted in the last presidential election. You would probably also be able to guess whether I prefer the *New Yorker* or *Glamour*, hot dogs or tofu, *Car Talk* or *Dr. Laura*, classical music or heavy metal. A person from Manhattan or San Francisco might feel greater cultural shock on a trip to Branson, Missouri, than they would in London.

This hunkering down with our own kind has an insulating, anesthetizing effect. As Bishop writes:

> Today we seek our own kind in like-minded churches, like-minded neighborhoods, and like-minded sources of news and entertainment. [And] like-minded, homogenous groups squelch dissent, grow more extreme in their thinking, and ignore evidence that their positions are wrong. As a result, we now live in a giant feedback loop, hearing our own thoughts about what's right and wrong bounced back to us by the television shows we watch, the newspapers and books we read, the blogs we visit online, and the neighborhoods we live in.

He cites a study that shows only 23 percent of Americans regularly talk politics among people with whom they disagree.

Social skills operate on the same principle as any other skills—you use 'em or you lose 'em. If you don't hang out regularly with people who are different from you, your ability to cope with these differences suffers. If living in homogenous neighborhoods isn't enough, technology makes it even easier to customize your existence. As Putnam writes in *Bowling Alone*, "Internet technology allows and encourages infrared astronomers, oenophiles, Trekkies, and white supremacists to narrow their circle to like-minded intimates. . . . Serendipitous connections become less likely as increased communication narrows our tastes and interests—knowing and caring more and more about less and less." Thousands of blogs and hundreds of television channels cater to every possible interest. Rather than listening to the radio, people shuffle their iPods or tune in to Internet radio sites like Pandora.com, which selects music geared to their tastes. Not only are we losing practice in relating to people who are different from us, but we as a nation have fewer cultural touchstones than we once did. The fragmentation of everything from politics to pop culture erodes our ability to deal with difference and keeps us from developing the shared stories and symbols that would make us feel that we're all in this together.

How to Be Polite

All the factors above have contributed to the increase in rudeness. Our time, energy, and budgets are sapped by increasing demands—from the workplace, from the ideology of intensive parenting, and from media-driven standards of appearance, fitness, and housekeeping—that leave us tired and cranky and too stressed to be polite. Increasing demographic diversity alienates us from our neighborhoods. The increasing lifestyle diversity (in everything from politics to pop culture) erodes our ability to deal with difference. And both kinds of diversity keep us from feeling that we're all in this together. It's a wonder we're not a whole lot ruder than we are, isn't it?

Plus, just as our motivation to be polite is on the downswing, the requirements for politeness have become ever more confusing. What does it even mean to be polite in the twenty-first century?

Certain kinds of rudeness—yakking loudly on cell phones in public places, undertipping, failing to RSVP—are obvious. But is standing when a woman enters the room respectful or sexist? Is forwarding a humorous e-mail a friendly way to keep in touch or the equivalent of spamming? Is telling someone you'll pray for them a kind way of indicating support or shoving your beliefs down their throat? Are locutions like "person of color" political correctness or plain courtesy? Is asking a coworker about her pregnancy a friendly show of concern or an invasion of privacy? You can find advocates for each point of view, all equally convinced that they alone are the true defenders of civility.*

Our society is in the midst of huge changes. The most notable is the movement of women, people of color, gays, and the disabled to full social equality. But there are other changes afoot, as well. Privacy norms, for example, are changing rapidly; talking about money or health was once a huge taboo, but people feel increasingly comfortable discussing their salaries, mortgages, colonoscopies, and cold sores. The explosion of information technology requires changes in manners: for hundreds of years, if you wanted to communicate with someone you couldn't speak to directly, you wrote to them. We got pretty good at letters and figured out what the form and manners of letter writing should be. Now there are cell phones and

---

* One rather hilarious Ali G sketch shows the ghetto youth in front of a sign reading "Respek" in bold Gothic lettering. Ali G intones solemnly, "Respek is important. But da sad t'ing is there's so little respek left in da world dat if you look up da word behind me in da dictionary, you'll find it's been taken out." I suspect that the reason many people feel that they're being disrespected today is because, like Ali G, they aren't looking in the right place.

text messages and blogs and instant messages and Skype and Twitter and Facebook, and there's an alarming chance that by the time we've figured out the form and manners for them, they'll be replaced by new technologies.

People handle cultural change in predictable ways, according to family historian Arlene Skolnick. When change begins, people initially see it as an individual affair. Maybe if they just worked harder things would be better. Maybe if they put their fingers in their ears and go "la la la," they won't be able to hear the sound of the gears shifting. When this kind of denial is no longer possible—when you come to realize that it's not just you, that cultural tectonic shift is afoot—social struggles begin. Some people are in favor of the change, others are not. This is where society is, for instance, with gay marriage right now. Finally, the culture restabilizes. What was once strange becomes normal. New rituals and manners get developed. And the kids? They'll grow up with it. And wonder and fight and adjust to whatever changes time has in store for their generation.

In the meantime, Miss Conduct can offer you guidance for living with "mind over manners" in the real world.

Just Who Do I Think I Am?

"[A]s a person of energy and resource, naturally fitted to dominate any situation in which she found herself, she vaguely imagined that such gifts would be of value to seekers after social guidance, but there was unfortunately no specific head under which the art of saying and doing the right thing could be offered in the market."

—Edith Wharton, *The House of Mirth*

When I was about three or four, some family friends gave me a magnetic letterboard—an item I already possessed. I opened my mouth and, as my mother cringed in fear for what I might say, piped up with perfect honesty and politeness: "Why, thank you! I just *love* these!"

You might think such a precocious moment of poise and consideration would have set me well on the way to a career as an etiquette columnist, but unfortunately the letterboard riposte was to be the apex of my social skills for many years to come. Unlike Judith Martin, Peggy Post, and Letitia Baldridge—you know, bona fide etiquette columnists—I did not grow up in elite social circles, imbibing D.C. protocol at the dinner table. I grew up in a series of Midwestern suburbs, where the dominant form of entertaining was the potluck dinner. And I grew up shy, the result of having about the longest "awkward stage" in the history of human development. (I have a PhD in human development, so I ought to know.)

The only good thing about being shy is that it gives you a lot of time alone to think about what life would be like if, indeed, you weren't. You rehearse all the things you'd do and say. I was lucky to break out of that prison of shyness, and by the time I did, I had some ideas of what I wanted to do with my freedom— one of which was to help keep others out of that prison, as much as I could, by helping them understand the skills and attitudes that eventually helped me escape.

The old saying "those who can't do, teach" is intended as a slur against all-theory-no-action academia, but there's a good bit of truth in it nonetheless. When you're very good at something, it is often so automatic, or so natural, that it can be hard to explain to others. Sometimes it can be easier to teach that which is difficult to do. I discovered this accidentally in graduate school when, even more accidentally, I was assigned to teach undergraduate statistics. As a mathphobe only barely in recovery,

I was dismayed—but, as it turned out, I was a *terrific* stats teacher. Why? Because I found the topic so difficult myself that I had to break it down and understand it at the most basic level. By the time I'd wrestled statistics down to the point that *I* could understand them, I could explain them to anyone.*

I can certainly "do" social skills these days—making small talk, negotiating awkward conversations, buying wedding presents: it's all in a day's work for me. But I remember when such things were agonizing trials. And I hope I can keep them from being so for you.

I don't think of myself as an authority—not if "authority" means someone who keeps people from having to think for themselves. I prefer to offer options and interpretations. I hope that my answers spark thought and discussion, not the smug sense of "Well, I know the rules now. Aren't I a good boy or girl?" But I'm definitely an authority in the sense of being an author—not just of a book but of my own life. I am the author of my choices, my priorities.

The goal of the next seven chapters is to help you take that sort of thoughtful responsibility for your own choices—to become the authority of your own life, as it were—in a social world that is in constant flux.

And to have a little fun along the way.

---

* And, unfortunately, still occasionally will at such inappropriate gatherings as cocktail parties and women's retreats at my synagogue. Once you've learned about z-score transformations it can be really hard to keep from sharing that knowledge.

· 1 ·

You Are What You Eat

FOOD

"Food is the first thing, morals follow on."*
—Bertolt Brecht, *The Threepenny Opera*

In Brecht's world of thieves, whores, and orphans, morality may have been a luxury only to be considered on a full belly, but moral questions in twenty-first-century America start well before you get to the table. Chicken or tofu? Grass-fed or corn-fed? Kosher or *trayf*? Imported organic or pesticide-sprayed local? And is "free-range" just another word for nothing left to lose? Then there are the questions that emerge not from morality but from health beliefs, social class, and individual taste. Carbs or fat? Frozen or fresh? Butter or margarine? Milk chocolate or dark? Etiquette books that tell you only which fork goes where on the table are taking the easy way out. The big question isn't where the forks go, but what the forks go *into*.

---

* Another popular translation from the original German, "First you must feed us, then we'll all behave," strongly suggests that the translator never hosted a children's birthday party.

I'm not going to make these choices for you. If I were living my perfect life, I would eat only food that was low-carb, low-fat, high-protein, cruelty-free, locally grown, organic, sugarless, kosher, and within my budget. Needless to say, this does not happen. It could, maybe, if I were willing to spend about 80 percent of my waking hours researching and acquiring things to eat. But however reasonable that way of life may have been for my hunter-gatherer ancestors, I have other things to do. So do you. We do the best we can, foodwise, on a rather feckless and ad hoc basis, cutting deals with our ideals here and there in order to get through life.

So how do we get along with those who cut different deals than we do—or with those few who do not, or cannot, allow any wiggle room in their food scruples?

In the very first draft of this chapter, I proceeded to launch into a jauntily confident list right about here. "Let's start with some basic definitions!" I chirped, after which I planned to provide quick and easy-to-remember descriptions of some of the more common types of food restrictions. "If you're having a vegetarian over for dinner, remember these three easy rules . . ."

Sadly, no.

Even among vegetarians, or observant Jews or Muslims, there is a tremendous spectrum of stringency, which opens your path onto at least two etiquette pitfalls: 1) Knowing that someone is a vegetarian, or keeps kosher or halal, doesn't tell you what to make for dinner next Saturday when she's coming over—except that it shouldn't be pork. 2) People within each of these food-rule communities (and many more, to boot) have wonderful fun pointing fingers, decrying that so-and-so doesn't *really* keep kosher or isn't *really* a vegetarian. Saying that someone isn't really what he says he is—or isn't really doing what he says he's doing—is *always* a great conversation starter at a dinner party.

Of course, there aren't just ethical or religion-based food restrictions; there are diabetes and celiac disease and alcoholism and all kinds of food allergies, too. According to the Food Allergy and Anaphylaxis Network, 90 percent of food allergies are caused by milk, eggs, peanuts, tree nuts, fish, shellfish, soy, and wheat—I mean, that's pretty much *food*, right there. That's what people *eat*, so of course it's going to cause difficulties. If humans developed allergies only to obscure edibles like lichen or truffles, there wouldn't be many problems, but that isn't how it usually works. I even know one poor soul who's allergic to corn. Take a tally of ingredient labels sometime: corn is in everything. It's like being allergic to hydrogen. And then there are the various fad diets, from Atkins to South Beach to *The Bible's Seven Secrets for Healthy Eating*, as well as more prosaic attempts to lower one's cholesterol or blood pressure. Would anyone ever insist that a neighbor treble his salt intake against doctor's orders for the sake of a midsummer night's barbecue?

Just to keep it simple, from here on out I'll refer to any and all such restrictions as "food rules." Whether food rules are based on health, ethics, religion, whim, or whatnot, here are the basic guidelines for dealing with them (yours and everyone else's) gracefully.

- **Other people's food rules.** Take people at their word. If someone says she can't eat shellfish, she can't eat shellfish. Maybe she thinks God doesn't want her to eat it, or maybe she knows for a painful fact that her immune or gastrointestinal system doesn't want her to do so. In either case, it's not a judgment on your shrimp-scarfing habits. She's not sitting there at the cocktail party deliberately *not eating shrimp at you.* So don't tempt or scoff or soliloquize about how, for you, life wouldn't be worth living without scampi. Chances are good if she doesn't eat shrimp, she doesn't particularly enjoy talking about shrimp, either.

• **Your own food rules.** Please don't make a liar out of me—be the person I described in the preceding paragraph! *Inform* people of what you can and can't eat, but don't try to *educate* them. Most people are fairly satisfied with their own eating habits and aren't looking to be reformed or enlightened. If someone complains of a health problem that you used to have until you stopped eating dairy, feel free to say, "You know, I used to have that problem, too, and when I stopped eating dairy it cleared up." Then shrug and add something like, "Everyone's body is different. Maybe it would work for you or maybe not." Keep the focus on your own experience; it's both more polite and more scientifically accurate to do so, and how often do you get to be both nice and empirically rigorous at the same time? Don't act like you're a better person because of your food rules—more spiritual, more ethical, more refined of palate. Maybe your food rules are, in fact, better than other people's, but nobody gets everything right; life's complicated. So don't sit there *not eating shrimp at someone.*

Why Food Rules?

WALLACE: "Won't you come in? We were just about to have some cheese."
WENDOLENE: "Oh no, not cheese. Sorry. Brings me out in a rash. Can't stand the stuff."
WALLACE [*gulp*]: "Not even Wensleydale?"
—Wallace and Gromit's *A Close Shave*

Thus was the great romance of Wallace and Wendolene scuppered. There are minefields around food etiquette, but why? Why is the fact that different people make different culinary choices not simply a matter of logistics? Why are emotions involved—why wouldn't Wallace just say, "More for me then! Come on in—I've got some biscuits, uncontaminated by cheese, that you might like"?

Negotiating food rules is both important and difficult because what and how we eat is tied in to our biology, our family history, our cultural values, our very identity. Our relationship with food is one of the major ways in which we define ourselves. It's not only people with food rules who have a "food identity." Deciding that you can and will eat anything—that's a food identity, too. We use food as props in the theater of our lives to show how refined (pinot noir), disciplined (salad with no dressing), sensual (scallops dripping in butter), educated (reverse-snobbery tap water instead of bottled), healthy (tofu), well-off (artisan cheeses), busy (takeout), successful (gourmet takeout), masculine (steak), feminine (chicken Caesar), worldly (ethnic food eaten with the proper protocol), adventuresome (fugu), or unpretentious (tuna casserole) we are.

This means that when you criticize someone else's food rules, even in such an implicit way as by not following them yourself, you are telling that person that some aspect of her identity is fundamentally *wrong*. Understandably, people get prickly about this. So it takes discipline to neither judge nor decide that you are being judged and come off all defensive about the Wensleydale.

Aside from people with medical restrictions, why do we have food rules, anyway? Koala bears don't have to ask themselves what to eat or when to eat it: the answer is eucalyptus, whenever they're awake. But humans are omnivores, which makes the question of what's for dinner a complicated one. We constantly have to make choices about what to eat. When you can potentially eat anything, you have to figure out which mushrooms to avoid and which to eat, which sea creatures are yummy and which might kill you. The individual can't possibly figure out what to eat and what not to eat on his own—the first wrong experiment might kill him. So one of the jobs of culture is to teach us what, when, and how to eat. This is the "omnivore's dilemma," a phrase coined by psychologist Paul Rozin in 1976 and popularized thirty years later by Michael Pollan, guru of the upscale-sustainable food set, in the title of his best-selling analysis of food consumption in modern America. (Humans aren't alone in this dilemma. Other omnivorous creatures, like baboons and monkeys and blackbirds, also watch their friends to learn which foods to eat, if not which forks to use.) Every culture settles on its own rules, based on a lot of different factors— the local crops, the local weather, the local sanitation system, the local religion.

Lots of people—including me, at times—advise people to listen to their bodies about what they should eat. This is good advice as far as it goes, but it's only going to go so far, I fear, because evolution has left us inclined to pay more attention to social and visual cues than to what our bodies tell us. As a species, we didn't "grow up" in a world of Big Macs and vending machines and food courts and more than two hundred kinds of breakfast cereal. We grew up not knowing where our next meal was coming from, and in the pre-refrigeration world the safest place to store "surplus" food was in our fat cells. So not only do we look to others to help us figure out what's good to eat, we don't have much of a sense of when to stop eating, either.

Some of the best research about humans' eating behavior has been conducted by Brian Wansink, a Cornell University professor and the executive director of the U.S. Department of Agriculture's Center for Nutrition Policy and Promotion (or, as I like to imagine him, the Pharaoh of the Food Pyramid). His book *Mindless Eating: Why We Eat More Than We Think* catalogs a series of thought- and laughter-provoking experiments into how much external cues, rather than internal ones (like hunger), drive our eating habits.

- Trying to get your kids to eat more vegetables? Rename a glass of vegetable juice "Rainforest Smoothie." When Wansink served Rainforest Smoothies to a Vacation Bible School class that was eating lunches in his kitchen/ laboratory, he ran out of the drink.* Four themes make food sound more appealing and can be found on most restaurant menus: geography (Tuscan Bean Soup); nostalgia (Wansink's rather weird example is "Green Gables Matzo Ball Soup"—who knew Anne Shirley was Jewish?); sensory (Succulent Prime Rib); and brand (Kobe Beef Burger).

---

* With so much acrimony over evolution these days, isn't it nice to see religion and science working together?

- Identical bottles of Charles Shaw Cabernet Sauvignon (the brand known among the cognoscenti as "Two-Buck Chuck") were given higher ratings when they were labeled "from a new California winery" than "from a new North Dakota winery." People receiving a complimentary glass of the "California" wine also ate more, and lingered more, over their dinner, which was mysteriously transformed into a special occasion.

- People are influenced not only by descriptions of food but by portion sizes. Why? Because we assume that the portion size we get is the portion size we're *supposed* to eat—that it's the social norm. Psychologically, "a serving" is however much fills the plate, the bowl, the glass, the bun, the bag. (We're also not very skilled in calculating in units smaller than whole numbers, so we don't generally take the step to figure out how much to eat of that one bag of chips that equals 2.5 USDA servings.)

- The presence of other people influences eating behavior. People faced with a plate of cookies will tend to eat as many as a "pacesetter," planted by the experimenter, eats. People who tend to eat a lot typically eat less in the presence of light eaters; those who don't eat much typically eat more when they're with diehard chowhounds. Eating with a crowd of seven or more will nearly *double* your food consumption—there is almost always someone eating, so you join them in empathetic nibbling.

- People also eat what they think is appropriate for their social position, including their gender. In one of the more entertaining studies, Wansink asked college students to read stories about a couple on a movie date. Only one detail differed in the stories: whether the man ate "almost all of his popcorn" or "a couple of handfuls." Male students thought the Heap Big Popcorn Muncher was significantly more aggressive and masculine—and could bench-press more!—than his more restrained counterpart. The female students were unimpressed by popcorn-eating prowess.

If you're thinking you would never fall for these silly food tricks, Wansink has also found that while no one will acknowledge that these social factors matter, nearly everyone behaves as though they do.

Breaking Sliced Bread

"Ninety percent of the diseases known to man are caused by cheap foodstuffs. You are what you eat."
—Beef advertisement, United Meet [*sic*] Markets, 1923

Food, then, contains both biological and social cues. We need to eat to fuel our bodies. But we also eat to fuel our relationships. As a social species, we eat together. We break bread to make peace, to welcome guests, to celebrate. We have special foods and drinks to mark special occasions (Thanksgiving turkey, Valentine's candy, Eid lamb, Diwali sweets, Sunday roast, congratulatory champagne). Needing food rules to keep us alive, we also find that they keep us together—and keep other people out. Some evolutionary psychologists believe that many food rules, such as keeping kosher, originated as a statement of tribal identity, a way of differentiating your group from others. (In *The Merchant of Venice*, Shylock memorably tells Bassanio: "I will buy with you, sell with you, talk with you, walk with you, and so following, but I will not eat with you, drink with you, nor pray with you." Business is secular; food is sacred). And once food rules take hold, they perpetuate segregation, because it is hard to eat with people who can't eat the same things you do, or who eat things you can't.

Or won't. Ask anyone who's converted to Judaism—like me—and they'll tell you the hardest thing isn't giving up Christmas, it's learning to eat gefilte fish.

What tastes good—and, even more important, what tastes "normal"—is shaped by all kinds of social factors. Chances are, if you could have a bumper sticker about it, it shapes how you eat. That encompasses religion, gender, ethnicity, political orientation, geographical region, educational level, interests, and hobbies, pretty much everything except your astrological sign—and while being a Virgo doesn't affect what you eat, being the kind of person who knows and cares that he is a Virgo probably would. Subcultures are routinely defined (and disparaged) by nonmembers in terms of their food habits: dog eaters, mackerel snappers, beaners, latte-sipping liberals, Joe Six-Pack, Cosmo girls. And one way to change your subculture is to change the way you eat. The first member of a family to go to college and join the professional class learns to drink microbrews and eat sushi. The children of immigrants learn to enjoy hamburgers and pizza—poignantly, they even learn to enjoy the Americanized fast-food versions of their native cuisine more than the real thing.

The existence of all of these different food subcultures—the sustainable/organic crowd eschewing big agribusiness, the ethnic-pride brigade cherishing old-country traditions, the dieters, the online gamers fueled by Slim Jims, Red Bull, and Doritos—is more noticeable in America than in other nations that have a more unified food culture. There are even those few dishes that are distinctly *American*, as you'll discover if you ever try to get a decent hamburger anywhere else in the world. We adopt the food of other countries into our own national cuisine as many countries do—after all, curry has become as English as pizza and chow mein are American, and one of the most famous Dutch dishes is rijstaffel, which is based on Indonesian cuisine.

Nearly any food is available to us—and, more strikingly, nearly any way of *relating* to food. We eat any hour of the night or day, and we eat any*thing* at any hour. We love to prohibit foods almost as much as we love to eat them. We Americans are prone to fad diets and have been ever since we became sufficiently prosperous, as a nation, to make choices about food rather than making do. This is because we don't have a strong food culture to oppose diets—really, can you imagine the Japanese or Italians going on a low-carb craze anytime soon? Also, in America, eating has increasingly become a solitary activity. Set mealtimes are squeezed out, and meals are increasingly eaten at desks and in cars. Because of this increased lack of coordination, we can individualize our food choices even more.

Supertaste me

Some of our most individualized food rules have their roots in our biology.

If you and your romantic partner (or your roommate) argue about the seasoning of food, try this the next time a fight is brewing. Take a break and drink a glass of milk, then look at your own and each other's tongues in a well-lit mirror. Chances are, whoever was arguing for less salt, sugar, or spice has a denser proliferation of taste buds on the tongue, which the thin coating of milk will reveal.

People differ in how many taste buds they have, and people who have more of them are more sensitive to taste. According to Linda Bartoshuk of Yale, about 25 percent of the population are "supertasters," who are more sensitive to strong flavors. Being a supertaster sounds like a good thing—we're Americans! we always want to be the best!—but supertasters don't have more refined palates, they just have a very low threshold for distinguishing tastes. They don't tend to desire fat and sugar as much as the rest of us, and they are often slimmer.

Interestingly, supertasters might be more sensitive overall and more emotionally reactive. Individual rats (who, remember, are omnivorous like us) who are highly sensitive to bitterness are generally more high-strung, and laboratory experiments suggest that human supertasters are more prone to anger and tension. So it might be best to let your supertaster mate win the argument over how much red pepper goes in the chili.

Scapegoat food

The biology of taste is important and somewhat startling. But differences in taste come more from individual learning than from the layout of your taste buds. Some of what you like and don't like derives from your own idiosyncratic experience of life.

A dramatic example is an aversion to a food you've eaten immediately before getting sick. Evolutionarily, this made sense. Why risk eating something that apparently made you sick the last time? People (and other omnivorous animals) are especially likely to form postnausea aversions to foods if they become sick after trying them for the first time. Vulnerable children and pregnant women are the most likely groups to develop food aversions. This is a good solution to a problem of evolutionary survival, but it's annoying when it kicks into overdrive and makes us shudder at the thought of a food that we know perfectly well wasn't responsible for making us sick. These aversions are learned in the gut, not the head. I had Korean barbecue for the first time right before coming down with the flu, and it will be a long time before I have it again.

Similarly, food aversions are a common reaction to chemotherapy. Some clever people will give chemo patients a "scapegoat food" with an unusual taste and minimal nutrition value—maple ice cream, say, or butterscotch candies—before treatment, so that the patients will start to hate that food and not something they encounter a lot and should continue to eat to keep up their strength.

Our learning starts early—even before birth. In one study, pregnant and breast-feeding women drank carrot juice for three weeks. The babies of both groups showed a much greater

✦ Learned food likes and dislikes aren't always dramatic events. I've taken a long voyage with ramen noodles. In college I lived on them because I was broke, and for years afterward I couldn't bear them. They tasted like deprivation. After about a decade of above-ramen-level income, I found I could tolerate them. Then I started keeping mostly a low-carb diet, which meant that noodles of any sort were a bit of a treat. Now a favorite snack (especially if I'm coming down with a cold) is a steaming bowl of ramen laced with sesame oil and red pepper flakes. Neither the chemistry of ramen noodles nor the biology of my sensory apparatus has changed, but the experience has: over twenty years, ramen noodles stopped tasting like bitter necessity and started tasting like forbidden fruit.

preference for carrots than your average tot does. Newborns exposed to bitter, sour formula—a flavor babies would normally hate—like it just fine at the age of seven months.

Comfort food

Families give us both nature and nurture—which means that our biological, environmental, and subcultural food factors gather, much like the guests at any cocktail or dinner party, in the family kitchen.

Taste preferences have a genetic component. But families inculcate many of our most emotional food beliefs and practices, whether these are explicitly communicated (like the fear of skipping a good breakfast) or implicitly passed on (like the idea that food equals love). Families teach us how much attention we are allowed to pay to our own bodies. Were individual tastes accommodated at the dinner table, or was everyone expected to eat what was put in front of him? Was the physical sensation of being full a sign to stop eating, or was there a plate-cleaning rule? Families teach us where food comes from: the farm, the grocery store, the kitchen, or the fast-food restaurant. Families teach us who is responsible for buying, cooking, and paying for food. They teach us which foods are appropriate for adults and for children, for men and for women, for every day and for special occasions. Families teach us whether we eat together or individually, whether a meal is a biological event or a social one.

For example, according to Food Pyramid Pharaoh Brian Wansink, men and women have very different notions of comfort foods: men prefer hot, meal-type foods like pasta, soup, and pizza, while women prefer ice cream, chocolate, and cookies. Mars and Venus? Not so fast. When he probed the reasons behind the difference, Wansink discovered that men's comfort foods reminded them of the foods mother used to make (subjects used words like "taken care of," "pampered," and "waited on" to express their emotional connection to the foods). Women, who identified with the mother in the kitchen, preferred no-hassle foods that didn't evoke memories of domestic labor.

Apparently soup is a lot less comforting when you're the one who has to cook it.

The "yummy" versus "not bad" distinction

Not liking something doesn't count as a food rule. Adulthood brings with it many privileges, such as being able to drive and stay up late at night. It also brings its attendant burdens, such as not being allowed to whine "This is gross!" at the table. Grown-ups can eat things they don't like and keep a pleasant face while doing it. Really, pause for just a moment and think about the fact that you get to eat pretty much *every time you are hungry*. Think how that compares to the experience of most people throughout human history. Think how it compares to the experience of many people living in the world today. Then, with that as a background, think, for a moment, about what breathtaking sense of entitlement it is to also demand that every meal you have be *yummy*.

That said, if you ever taste something bad—I don't mean bad, I mean *bad*—you must *spit it out immediately*. As discreetly as possible, of course, but immediately. It may be embarrassing, but my husband once got hepatitis from giving a questionable clam the benefit of the doubt. Red cheeks for ten seconds are better than a green face for half a year. And in any situation, food related or not, every time you overcome embarrassment in order to do the sensible thing, you give others just a little bit of courage to do the same.

Being a Good Guest with Personal Food Rules

Question: *I've such a sensitive allergy to seafood that even touching shellfish, or touching someone who's recently handled shellfish, can cause a potentially deadly reaction. Since shrimp and crab hors d'oeuvres are popular at functions, I'm stumped when someone extends a hand to shake. Many times, I've declined shaking hands with a brief explanation of my allergy. A coworker recently suggested begging off the handshake by explaining I have a cold, but I think that makes me sound a bit paranoid. How do I handle the situation without sharing my medical history?*

So let's say you're living with serious food rules—not just preferences, such as disliking Wensleydale or preferring to eat locally grown produce—but the kind of food rules that come with a lifelong medical condition or ethical/religious commitment. Perhaps the restrictions of your diet feel like a chore to you; perhaps they feel like a joy. What is your chore, in either case: explaining your situation to others when necessary.

- **Don't be coy.** Whether your food rules are the result of choice or necessity, there are far too many types of food rules out there for you to expect others to pick up on subtle or even not-so-subtle but indirect signals. Not everyone knows that a diagnosis of diabetes can mean avoiding not just sugars and candies but also main-course and "healthy" foods such as white flour, potatoes, carrots, peas, and cottage cheese (and that's far from a complete list). Lots of kosher-keepers will cheerfully tell others that they can't eat "bottom-feeding" fish or fish without scales, in the blissful idea that this clarifies matters for others. A significant number of Americans, particularly those who grew up in the middle of the country, think of fish as white rectangles in the grocer's freezer section. (Until I was in my teens I didn't even know fish came with or without scales; I just thought they came with or without breading.)

• **Embrace the awkwardness of food rules.** If you're mortally allergic to shellfish, don't feel embarrassed to say, "I'd love to shake hands, but I have a serious allergy and can't touch anyone who might have touched the crab cakes. So, what did you think of the keynote speaker?" Sure, it's moderately awkward, and it will be tiresome to have to repeat it. But any medical condition involves annoyances— some physical, some social. Take the occasional social awkwardness as one of the symptoms of your allergy and deal with it as you would any irritating symptom: alleviate it as much as possible and do your best to ignore what you can't help. Besides, by mentioning your allergy, you are educating others that such allergies exist. Imagine how nice it would be for you if, halfway through your little recitation, the person you were speaking with said, "Oh, sorry! Last week, I met someone who has the same thing with peanuts. Must be a real pain. Anyway, what did you think of the keynote speaker?"

• **Make communicating food rules into a habit.** Don't assume that because you've communicated your food rules to someone once, they're going to be able to remember them and get them right the next time. Until your way of life becomes as much a habit for others as it is for you, they'll make mistakes. Don't take the occasional faux pas as an insult or covert attempt to bring you over to the dark side. It probably took you a while to remember your own food rules, if you didn't grow up with them from your early childhood. Sure, some people may "forget" your food rules out of thoughtlessness or disrespect, but most people honestly *forget*; we live in an age of information overload, and people forget all kinds of things. (My agent, marketing person, editor, and mother still occasionally refer to my *Boston Globe* column as "Miss Manners," for example.)

• **Don't be wishy-washy about what you can and can't eat.** People with food rules sometimes think that it's polite to be open-ended about menu options, but that leaves your host not knowing what to do, which is unfair. If someone is preparing food for you, be specific and directive in explaining what and how you can eat. If you're invited to dinner and the host doesn't ask if you have any restrictions, volunteer them. And if your rules are somewhat complex—like keeping kosher, as opposed to being allergic to seafood—it might be easier to explain your rules in terms of what you *can* have rather than what you can't. (Alternatively, you could ask the host what he plans on serving and let him know if it works for you.) If you're restricted from something that works its way into other foods—like sugar or gluten—alert your host to this and give examples of the biggest food hazards for you.

• **Recognize that not every situation may be able to accommodate you.** Depending on the stringency and breadth of your food rules, it may be simple to rejigger a menu to fit your rules, but, if it isn't, don't take it as a personal insult. Either decide not to attend the pig roast or eat beforehand and enjoy the tropical rum punch. You can also ask the host if it's all right for you to bring your own food.

Not all food rules are lifelong. Maybe you just have to stay away from certain foods for a while until your doctor has figured out what's making your gut go blooey. Or perhaps you're on a diet, or maybe it's Ramadan or Lent. Don't inconvenience others with a temporary change of diet, if you can at all help it; by the time they finally get straight what you can and can't have, you'll be back to your usual level of omnivorance. If you're fasting or abstaining from particular goodies for a religious reason, the whole point is that it's supposed to be a pain in your butt, so don't go making it a pain in anyone else's. If it's a temporary medical restriction, declining with a simple "I just ate, thanks" is often an easier solution than going into a long explanation of what your gastroenterologist thinks is going on with your innards. Do what you can to take control of the situation by inviting people to your house, or suggesting restaurants that you know will have food you can eat.

Being a Good Guest with Public Food Rules

"So much about life in a global economy feels as though it has passed beyond the individual's control—what happens to our jobs, to the prices at the gas station, to the vote at the legislature. But somehow food still feels a little different. We

can still decide, every day, what we're going to put into our
bodies, what sort of food chain we want to participate in."
—Michael Pollan, *The Omnivore's Dilemma*

I've been talking a great deal, so far, about the idea that one
person's food rules aren't a judgment on another's and shouldn't
be taken as such. But what if your food rules aren't the result of
personal medical conditions or private religious/ethical commitments, but reflect moral principles you do in fact believe everyone
should uphold?

There are vegetarians who believe no one should eat meat,
period, and environmentalists who believe no one should eat
food that has more frequent-flier miles than Bono. These are reasonable, thoughtful positions, yet you can't go around aggressively and argumentatively proselytizing or people will think
you're an annoying kook. "I don't care what people think of me
as long as I know I'm doing the right thing!" you declare. Well,
if they think you are an annoying kook, then they will think
vegetarianism or environmentalism are the kinds of ideas held
by annoying kooks, and that doesn't do your earth-saving plan
very much good, now does it? Better they should think of you
as a fun person with boundless energy and glowing skin who
brings amazing vegan cookies into the office on the last Friday
of every month or is willing to pick up an extra pint of straw-
berries for them at the farmers' market.

When your moral convictions don't jibe with the behavior of
practically anyone you know, it's vital to your sanity to draw a line
between your public and private life. (This is true for many issues
besides food, obviously.) Concentrate your efforts on getting
everyone to behave better in the public sphere. Work politically

for good farm policies, more accurate nutritional guidelines, better school lunches, community-supported agriculture, animal welfare—whatever your particular deep ethical commitments are—but don't preach at your friends and neighbors.

Being a Good Host to the Food Ruled

So your peanut-allergic kid's new playdate partner has celiac disease, or your South Beach–devoted best friend is dating a fruitarian, or your roommate develops high blood pressure, or the new guy in your cube farm is a devout garlic-free Buddhist— or you're an up-and-coming, meat-loving chef hosting all five of them at once on the wacky new sitcom *Vegan Zombies Eat Your Graaaaaaains*. What courtesies does the carnivorous host owe her vegan guests (besides not eating them)?

- **Ask questions!** Not nosy questions aimed at satisfying your morbid curiosity, but practical ones that will tell you what you need to know to figure out what to have for dinner, how to share refrigerator space, or whatever.* If the food rules are serious and complex, and you're going to be sharing food space and time with this person, take notes. Don't be afraid to ask follow-up questions if you don't understand the rules. Even if you do understand them, ask a confirming follow-up question, such as "Okay, so you can't eat wheat. No pasta and no bread, but what else has wheat gluten that I wouldn't necessarily think of?"

---

* If your roommate also happens to be your romantic partner, nosy questions that satisfy your morbid (and loving) curiosity are always fair game.

- **Reveal mistakes.** If you mix 'n' mess up while you're cooking for, or sharing food space with, someone who has food rules, tell her—even if she'd never know otherwise. It won't be the first mistake she's ever encountered, and she'll be glad you treated her with respect instead of keeping silent and that you put her comfort and autonomy above your desire to save face.

- **Don't judge.** If your food-ruled friend, relative, or colleague falls off the wagon now and then, keep your mouth shut about it. People vary in how strictly they observe their food rules. I've known good vegetarians who, once or twice a year, sneak out for a big blowout of barbecued pork ribs, and I bet those ribs taste a whole lot better to them than they would to us carnivores. Some people with allergies occasionally decide that the deliciousness of the mango is worth the rash. And some folks who keep mostly kosher maintain a "don't ask, don't tell" policy about dim sum. Don't tease or even comment when someone sneaks a forbidden treat, as long as you're sure they're doing it on purpose and not because they've made a mistake about the ingredients.

- **Ask more questions!** It's okay, once you get to know someone, to ask about his food rules for curiosity-satisfying purposes. But since food rules are usually based on health, religion, or ethics—extraordinarily personal topics—first ask if you may ask. (You'll find more detailed guidelines for how to ask thoughtful and appropriate questions about health and religion in their respective chapters.) Don't ask if the person misses the food he can't eat, or praise his discipline, or treat him as exotic. Don't try to argue him out of his food rules, or insist that he "just try" something. This is the case no matter how old or young the person is, or whether you yourself "believe in" peanut allergies or the Koran or not. You don't have to believe in the Koran: you only have to believe in people's right to decide for themselves what they will put in their own bodies.

Treating people's food rules with respect also doesn't require that you follow the rules yourself. (Not usually, anyway. If allergies are bad enough that a person might not be able to be in the same room as the allergen, you might have to restrain yourself—but that's pretty rare.) Don't feel self-conscious about eating something that another person can't have. Ask him if he minds, and believe him if he says he doesn't. Nature is kind that way; if you don't eat something for a long time, you eventually lose the taste for it. The one exception is McDonald's french fries.

People over Food

When you're fixing dinner for one or two friends, it's easy enough to find out their preferences and adjust the menu accordingly. But what about larger events? Let's start by taking some of the scare element out of entertaining, because we seem to be frightening ourselves out of doing it.

In *Bowling Alone*, Robert Putnam documents a steep decline in dinner parties since the 1970s. I wonder if this decline in entertaining is partly the result of great expectations about how fancy entertaining is supposed to be. Back in the day, a deck of cards, a few bowls of potato chips, a bottle of gin, and some ice would get you through a pleasant night with friends. It still would, if you could banish the specter of Martha Stewart from your mind. Or propitiate the specter by designating your evening as a themed "Retro '50s Card Party"—harking back to Brian Wansink's advice on the power of labeling.

The point of a dinner party is to have good conversation with interesting people over food. That's *people* over *food*, get it? The "dinner" is but an excuse for the "party." Stop worrying about the food so much, in other words, and pay more attention to your guest list. (Much the same principles apply to the guest list and the menu: balance tastes and texture,. the spicy and the sweet, the crunchy and the bland. Quality is more important than quantity. Try to combine a few elements you know well and a few that are relative unknowns.) If you like cooking, it's never a sin to enjoy impressing your guests with your mad skills. If you're a less ambitious chef, experiment around a bit until you've found a menu that's easy and that everybody likes. Then make it your signature dish and keep serving it. Your guests won't mind; look how many people order the same thing every time they go to a favorite restaurant, after all.

Don't listen to entertaining guidebooks that prize perfection over chutzpah. Such books often say you should make a new dish for practice before serving it to company, to ensure that it will turn out right on the big night. This is nonsense. If you're not comfortable enough with your guests to say, "Major kitchen disaster—we'll be sending out for pizza!" why did you invite them in the first place? For less unambiguous disasters, confidence can carry you through a lot. A wonderful cook of my acquaintance once told me, "If you're having people over for dinner and a dish doesn't turn out quite as you'd planned, never apologize. Your guests don't know what it was *supposed* to taste like, and chances are they'll be perfectly happy as long as they think they should be."

For a high-stakes event, with clients or bosses or the like, either take people out to a restaurant or hire a caterer. If the party is that socially and professionally important, you don't want to be stuck in the kitchen, anyway.

Now that we've taken the nervy bits out of cooking for ordinary guests, let's talk about those who are just a little bit trickier—your guests with food rules. The most important thing is communication. When you issue your invitation, ask people if there is anything they do not eat. Although, obviously, don't ask it in those words, or it might come across, "Is there *anything* you don't eat?!" I suggest the line, "Please let me know if there are any foods to which you have ethical, allergic, or aesthetic objections." It's corny, but the semi-alliteration makes it stick in people's minds, which means they'll actually remember to tell me when they RSVP.

If you wind up having a number of people with food restrictions, do a buffet in which everyone can eat at least three things, at least one of which is a source of protein.* And always, at a buffet dinner or party-with-nibbles, label the food unless it's clear what exactly it is. Pay special attention to hidden ingredients that might cause people distress—dairy, wheat, nuts, alcohol, and so forth. Labeling is helpful not only for people who might want to avoid forbidden foods, but also for people who just like to

---

* I find that soul food prepared in a health-conscious style is a surprisingly versatile cuisine for buffet dinners and provides a lot of variety when you're dealing with a mixed group. A favorite menu of mine is baked chicken drumsticks, collard greens with black beans or lentils, vegetarian dirty rice, baked squash and tofu, corn muffins, and salad. Recipes in the appendix!

know what they're eating. Label things that are spicy, too, or else you'll spend the entire evening launching yourself across the room to inform people that those olives are stuffed with jalapeños, like I did on one New Year's Eve.

There are many kinds of accommodations that can be made for guests with food rules, and sometimes it's the guests who need to accommodate the host and accept a less-than-optimal dining experience for the sake of fellowship. There are no hard-and-fast rules for what a reasonable accommodation is or isn't: it depends on the size of the gathering, the host's resources, the advance ("R&D") time between invitation and eating, the extent to which a particular food is the entire point of the gathering (just *don't go* to the bake-off if you have celiac disease), how complicated the food rules are, and the possibilities of other eating options.

One rule always applies: if you're making people travel several hours to your wedding reception, you pretty much have to feed them something they can eat.

· 2 ·

Mad (About) Money

FINANCES

"The love of wealth is . . . at the bottom of all that the Americans do . . . It perturbs their minds, but it disciplines their lives."

—Alexis de Tocqueville

People are destined never to agree about money. There are scrimpers and savers and spenders and splurgers. There are people who have more and those who have less. There are those who love money and those who hate it and those who love money only when it loves them in return. And among all of these individuals with different circumstances and temperaments, there are rich opportunities for social awkwardness and unintended insult.

You can go back to George Eliot, or Shakespeare, to see these problems play out. What makes money manners especially tricky now is the collision between the belief that money should be private and the incessant publicizing of it. We watch several twenty-four-hour cable channels to track financial news to help us gauge—to the minute if we like—how much money we'll have (or not have) in our retirement accounts. At an Internet click, we can discover how much our neighbors and friends spent on their houses and whether they took out second mortgages. We can pick up a magazine and learn, as never before, the lifestyles of the wealthy, including the designer labels they favor for their newborn babies (and which are portrayed as middle-class normalcy, leaving us to wonder why *we* don't have those things). Thirty-second news reports on worldwide rice shortages are followed by thirty-second commercials for luxury cruise lines or loyalty-program credit cards that promise escape into a world of unparalleled indulgence. People are striving to cope with personal debt, national debt, crumbling infrastructure, and crumbling job security— along with a constant message that it is both our right and our responsibility to shop, look good, feel good, and play hard.

Twenty-first-century American money culture is a textbook example of cognitive dissonance and mixed messages, so it's no wonder everyone feels a bit weird and awkward. To understand how to behave with modern financial grace, we have to get to the heart of what money means.

Dog Eat Dog

"A dog has no use for fancy cars or big homes or designer clothes. Status symbols mean nothing to him."

—John Grogan, *Marley and Me*

As any dog lover will recognize immediately, the first and second sentences of that quote have nothing to do with one another. Of course dogs don't care about whether their collars display the trendy new color of the season or whether they're drooling out the window of a Lexus or a barely running beater—and they definitely don't have any sense of the kind of

high-end consumer goods that writing a best seller as monumental as *Marley and Me* can net a fortunate writer. (Though I'm
not sure it's accurate to say dogs have no "use" for status symbols. I'm sure my dog Milo could while away many a happy
hour lying on Pratesi sheets gnawing on a pair of Christian
Louboutin shoes.)

But that doesn't mean dogs are immune to status: they, like
all social animals, are *obsessed* with it. Anyone who has wit-
nessed a Jack Russell striving mightily to pee higher on the tree
than the Great Dane who was there before him can see that. But
the conjoined facts that dogs are status-obsessed creatures, yet
we modern humans sentimentally prefer to pretend they're not,
gets at the heart of why money is among our most vexing issues.

Like dogs, humans are social animals, evolved to both cooperate and compete with our fellows. We cooperate to obtain
resources; we compete to make sure we get our fair share—and,
ideally, just a wee bit more than our fellows—of said resources
once obtained. But as highly intelligent primates, we, unlike
dogs, conduct our status wars in symbolic languages: goods,
personal adornment, job titles, McMansions. The human vo-
cabulary of power extends far beyond peeing and humping.*

Even in situations where physical force is the most readily
available source of status, we'll create symbolic means of exchange. Take, for instance, the booming demand for mackerel
in the federal prison system. According to the *Wall Street Journal*, oily pouches of "macks" are the currency of choice for prisoners, who aren't allowed to have cash (or cigarettes, the
previous currency of choice). Mackerel pouches are an efficient
wealth marker because: "few—other than weight-lifters craving

---

* And no, exceptions won't be discussed in this book.

protein—want to eat it," and thus no one is at great risk of can-
nibalizing their own stash.

Macks, markers, or dollars: we'll turn anything into *money*,
however conflicted we are about our cravings for it. Evolutionarily, we can't help but want to compete *and* cooperate. We
simultaneously want to be recognized as king of the hill and one
of the gang. We feel that there is something wrong with wanting
to keep up with the Joneses, yet we are jonesing to outshine
them nonetheless. As a study by Sara Skolnick and David
Hemenway shows, most people would rather earn $50,000 a
year in a world where everyone else makes $25,000 than earn
$100,000 in a world of $200,000 earners.* It's not how much
you have, it's how much you have *relative to everyone else* that
makes you feel all warm inside. That's not the way human nature is supposed to work according to Jesus, Aesop's fables, or
even traditional economics, but that's how it is.

Money and status are especially tricky to negotiate in the
United States, where 53 percent of people describe themselves
as "middle class"—including some people with household incomes under $20,000 and others with incomes over $150,000.
If you also scoop up the people who identify themselves as
"upper middle class" or "lower middle class," a whopping 91
percent of Americans are self-styled members of the middle. We
want to believe that we're all more or less on the same team. According to sociologist Alan Wolfe, Americans are determined to
be middle class because "unlike being poor, being middle class

---

* They found similar results for attractiveness and intelligence of one's self and
one's child, too—that is, people would rather have a semi-cute kid in a world of
ugly children than an averagely cute kid in a world of Gerber babies, and so on.
Most of us, it would seem, wouldn't mind at all being the one-eyed king of the
blind.

means earning enough to have some choice about where and how to live. . . . Unlike being rich, to be middle class is to believe that what one has achieved is due not solely to family advantage—although within reason that is never to be spurned—but to one's own hard work and efforts." We want to see ourselves in the flattering glass of the middle class: a virtuous earner, neither victim nor vulture.

At the same time that we want to be "just folks," Americans want to be rich, as the Tocqueville quote at the beginning of this chapter illustrates. Almost two hundred years later, *New York Times* columnist and pop sociologist David Brooks opined that in the lives of his infamous *BoBos in Paradise*, "the big money stream is another aptitude test. Far from being a source of corruption, money turns into a sign of mastery," and wealth denotes your expertise and intellect. Some of us even believe God, that ultimate arbiter of the pure and the corrupt, wants us to be rich, as the best-selling *The Prayer of Jabez: Breaking Through to the Blessed Life*, the *Harry Potter* of the "prosperity gospel" movement, demonstrates.

Of late, Americans' aspirations for middle-class fellowship and upper-class triumph have taken a beating. Economists are nearly unanimous that since the 1970s income inequality in the United States has grown enormously, and the twenty-first century has gotten off to a rocky start for all but the very wealthiest.* According to a 2008 Pew Research Center poll—conducted before the announcement in the year's fourth quarter that the economy was officially in recession—31 percent of middle-class Americans said that life is worse for them than it

---

* "Near" unanimity is as good as it gets in the social sciences. Humans aren't uniform, after all—precisely why our interactions can get so slippery.

had been five years earlier, and 25 percent said they were "hold-ing steady," the highest response to this question in the forty-four years it had been asked. More than half the families in the survey reported having to cut back on expenditures in the previous year; a quarter were worried about layoffs, outsourcing, or company relocation, and about the same number feared salary and bene-fits cutbacks. A 2007 Demos survey reported that over half of all middle-class households had no net assets—no nest egg—whatsoever. A quarter were at risk of dropping out of the middle class entirely.

A terrifying book by financial reporter Steven Greenhouse, *The Big Squeeze: Tough Times for the American Worker*, offers a closer look at the financial plight of Americans. He writes, "The squeeze on the American worker has meant more poverty, more income inequality, more family tensions, more hours at work, more time away from the kids, more families without health insurance, more retirees with inadequate pensions, and more demands on govern-ments and taxpayers to provide housing assistance and health coverage." Here are some of his easy-to-choke-on findings:

- Hourly earnings for 80 percent of American workers have risen only 1 percent since 1979, adjusting for inflation, while worker productivity has risen by 60 percent.
- If wages had kept pace with productivity, the average full-time employee would be earning $58,000 a year instead of the 2007 average of $36,000.
- For people between ages twenty-five and thirty-four, mortgage debt nearly doubled between 1983 and 2007.
- It's not just money, it's time: professional workers are routinely faced with fifty-plus hours a week at work, while

wage workers are often forced to do mandatory overtime—
on or (illegally) off the clock.

As these statistics make clear, that vast middle class has reason
to feel insecure about money—and as the emotion expert Paul
Ekman has noted, a fearful mood often primes us to behave more
emotionally, to more readily act or respond with anxiety or de-
fensiveness. All of us, Jack Russells and Great Danes alike, are
facing anxious times. Can we do something more productive
with our anxieties than pee on the neighbors' bushes?

Money Talks

Question: *My husband and I make modest salaries and
lead an unassuming middle-class life. Our three children,
however, are the beneficiaries of a generous trust fund established by their grandparents. Recently, we have decided
to tap into the fund to send our youngest to a private school
known for its staggering tuition. Friends and acquaintances
cannot help but ask how we can afford it. How can I respond
without revealing the trust fund, which my own children do
not yet know about?*

One thing you can do when you feel weird about money is
not talk about it and hope that it goes away—the weird feeling,
that is, not the money itself. Another thing is to ask around to
see if you're the only one who's feeling that way.

During much of the twentieth century, the official rule about
discussing money was simple: nice people didn't. In 1942, Emily
Post commanded, in no uncertain terms, "A very well-bred man

intensely dislikes the mention of money and never speaks of it (outside of business hours) if he can help it." Nondisclosure on money, sex, and religion was de rigueur. For two out of the three topics, the rule was completely unsustainable. Money and sex are incredibly *interesting*, and nearly everyone is anxious because they suspect they're not getting quite as much as everyone else. So people have started talking numbers again.

This free and frank money talk may, however, signal a return to the older folkways rather than a bold new direction. For instance, a 2007 *New York Times* article notes, "I've often wondered how it was that the characters in Jane Austen's novels always seemed to know everyone else's income. By the time you're on the second page of *Pride and Prejudice*, you hear that a young man named Mr. Bingley is about to move into the neighborhood and that his income is £5,000 a year. Later when Mr. Darcy, the romantic lead of the book, makes his entrance, you quickly learn that his income is £10,000 a year." Because of this evidence, some literature and history professors maintain that people knew darned well what everyone else worth back in the day. All they had to do was look up their neighbors' net worth in the land register and find the husband of their daughters' dreams.

The once-inviolable rule of "no money talk"—like that earlier tradition of predatory matchmaking—has been abandoned. Today, nice people do talk about money and, as with sex, the talk can get quite graphic. So it's important to learn how to mindfully conduct your money talk.

- **Learn your own comfort level.** When someone asks you a financial question you'd rather not answer, just say, "Oh,

I don't discuss money." You're not judging them; you're just stating your own boundaries.

- **Listen for the question behind the question.** Perhaps your friend doesn't really want to know about you and your finances per se but instead is wondering about a reasonable rent for a house in your neighborhood, whether the salaries at your company are competitive because he's applying for a job there, or if you feel you're getting your money's worth out of your kid's college. If that is the case, recommend resources: "I don't like to talk about my own finances, but I can say that this is generally a pretty reasonable neighborhood, rentwise—I can send you the contact information for the rental agent I used, if you want."

- **Don't act offended or disgusted if someone shares tales of financial adventures.** Money talk is just numbers; it doesn't have the squirm- and squeam-inducing property of unwanted medical or sexual information. Still, you needn't feel obliged to reciprocate with a revelation of your own. (Reciprocation is a conversational norm, but "norm" means "most of the time," not "always," conveniently enough.) Instead, ask a question that will take the numbers out of the conversation: "And do you also get good vacation time at the new job? Planning any trips?" or "It's a beautiful house. Have you met any of your new neighbors yet?"

- **Avoid pronouncing that an amount is a lot or a little (unless it's obvious).** "I got this dress for $125!" doesn't tell you if $125 is a lot for your coworker to spend on a dress or a terrific bargain. If you value financial discretion, then don't give your own spending standards away with your reaction: "That's a great find" works in either situation. (In some cases, people will seek you out *because* you are knowledgeable about the market. But just because your coworker wants to confess buyer's remorse doesn't mean she wants you to confirm that she made a foolish purchase.) Of course, there will be times when the person tells you if it's a lot or a little, or when it's incredibly obvious: "I bargained the guy down to $5,000 for the Lexus, and he even threw in a free GPS!" In that case, follow her lead.

- **If you're deeply private about money, it's time to realize that the Internet has made things a lot tougher.** Just as anyone can look up how much you paid for your house, they can also uncover your political campaign contributions and the average salaries for your profession. You don't have control over much of that information, and if information is out there for the getting, people will go out and get it. You'll simply have to relax about it.

- **If you like to talk openly about money, recognize that not everyone does.** Maybe you think they should, but you're not going to get adherents by making people uncomfortable. Mention your own information first and see how the conversation progresses. If the other person responds in vague hand wavings rather than hard numbers, then clearly she has different feelings about financial disclosure. Move the conversation from the quantitative to the qualitative, pronto.

One group of people with whom you should always talk openly about your finances is your children. They don't need to know every detail of your second mortgage or when your CDs mature, but kids *notice* things. They notice if your car is a lot older, or newer, than the other ones on the block. They notice where other kids go on vacation over spring break. They notice whether the breakfast cereal is name-brand or generic. So it's only fair to explain to them the underlying reasons behind these things.

Plus, it's in your own self-interest. When the finances of the house are shrouded in secrecy, kids can come to believe there is something taboo about money: that it is shameful, mysterious, and out of their control. Kids who are taught that money is "grown-ups' business" are less likely to know how to manage their own money when they grow up. And people who don't learn how to make their own financial decisions are more likely to turn to their parents for help well into adulthood, whether that means living with their parents or tapping them for "loans" that may not be paid off for decades. If you dream of a well-lined and *empty* empty nest, make sure your kids are financially literate. A slow economy or personal misfortune might keep adult children financially dependent for a lot longer than either they or their parents want. You can't control that, so take control over what you can: how much financial education and self-determination you bestow on your kids.

Kids should know what the family financial situation is: where the money comes from, how much it is, and where it goes. And *why*.

The Value(s) of Money

"Well, whiles I am a beggar, I will rail
And say there is no sin but to be rich;
And being rich, my virtue then shall be
To say there is no vice but beggary."
—William Shakespeare, *King John*, act 2, scene 1

Some people seek status through material wealth, others through freedom from being concerned with it. Every subculture has its own status symbols—hybrid cars, travel to India, Cristal champagne, hired limousines, vintage bowling shirts, season tickets to the symphony, bottled water, rejection of bottled water, jeans costing more than a hundred dollars, RVs, organic six-hundred-thread-count sheets—that don't translate in other subcultures. The diamond jewelry and designer tracksuits that scream status to one person scream hopeless vulgarity to another. Clothes worn well past their fashion prime may signal poverty, a commitment to reduce environmental impact, an old-fashioned WASP ethos of thrift, or a feminist rejection of media-driven beauty standards. Keeping a vegetable garden can be an expensive luxury or a money-saving necessity.

In some ways, it's easier to be friends with someone who has a lot more, or a lot less, money than you do than it is to be friends with someone who has about the same amount but very different values. Which is probably why so few people manage it. If you're a radical Dumpster-diving freegan who bikes everywhere less than twenty miles away and hasn't bought new clothes since college, you probably won't be friends with a wine-obsessed audiophile who's still paying off that massaging recliner from Brookstone and who won't leave the house without the right designer product in his hair. And if you're a wine-obsessed audiophile who's still paying off that massaging recliner from Brookstone and won't leave the house without the right designer product in your hair, you'll probably soon discover strains in your friendship with a diligent bargain chaser who will spend a full day finding a fifty-dollar discount on a power suit and who believes that carrying over a credit card balance is a moral failing. If you manage to nurture such friendships, it's only going to be because you've established a bond of trust and respect—and a sense of humor about it all.

Despite their appearances, these very different personalities— to save myself some typing, let's give them the cheesy but gender-neutral monikers Freegan Phil, Material Mel, and Supersaver Sam—can all be earning about the same amount of money. In *spending* their money, they're displaying very different inner values and priorities—but that behavior may be the product of life circumstances as well. It's easier for a Freegan Phil to embrace what psychologists call "post-materialist" values if Phil obtained a college education, enjoys generally good health, holds a job that doesn't require image maintenance, and can access emergency funds if needed. In short, it's relatively easy to live as though you are broke (or to actually be broke) as long as you can tap into sufficient social and cultural capital to avoid the real, awful experience of being poor. A Material Mel may work in a profession in which appearance, hair-product-dependent though it may be, is a significant asset, and in which being able to discuss Bose and Beaujolais is how you make yourself part of the gang. Or Mel may work in a law firm that insists women wear heels and hose as part of their professional attire and may spend more on makeup and general grooming than someone who works in a biotech lab. And the conscientiousness so prized by a Supersaver Sam might be an attempt to recover from a college-age credit binge or to ensure that she doesn't suffer the same deprivations as her struggling, working-class single mother did.

One person's luxury may be another's necessity, or something close to it. People may feel the need to buy houses beyond their means in order to get their kids into a good public school, and they may be prohibited by their housing association from useful money-saving activities like planting vegetable gardens or hanging clotheslines. Certain kinds of frugality require the privilege of good health, spare time, and relative freedom from having to make an impression on others. Not everyone has these blessings in abundance.

Which is why it's complicated to interpret the connections between *stuff* and happiness—and to figure out how to conduct yourself around friends and money to maximize the latter.

Material Happiness

There's nothing wrong with stuff, in itself. It's our attitudes toward stuff that cause the problems. Materialism can best be understood (at least by social scientists) as a constellation of values, including a desire for money and stuff and a preoccupation with image, personal appearance, fame, and social status. Studies by multiple researchers on people of both genders, of all ages, and in many different countries all converge on the point that materialism does not make us happy.

But do materialistic values make people unhappy or does happiness (based on good health, a strong community, and a quality education) enable people to transcend materialism? Like many relationships, the one between materialism and happiness probably goes in both directions. For example, materialism correlates with depression and anxiety, as well as headaches, backaches, muscle soreness, and sore throats (good thing Material Mel has that massaging recliner). A Material Mel is likely to be more conformist, feel as though he's playing a role rather than being himself, and feel less autonomous and free than Freegan Phil.

This last bit is because materialism by definition focuses on external rewards rather than the internal ones. External rewards, ultimately, don't make people happy. According to Alfie Kohn, author of *Punished by Rewards: The Trouble with Gold Stars, Incentive Plans, A's, Praise, and Other Bribes*, external rewards can be bad *even if you're originally motivated from within*. If you get paid to do the thing you love, the theory goes, then you'll start to believe you're doing it only for the money—and that will ultimately lead you into the role of self-fulfilling prophet. Or, in the words of that great American prophet Mark Twain: "There are wealthy gentlemen in England who drive four-horse passenger-coaches twenty or thirty miles on a daily line, in the summer, because the privilege costs them considerable money; but if they were offered wages for the service, that would turn it into work and then they would resign."

Does this mean that your only option in the pursuit of a happy, rewarding life is the camaraderie of the starving artist—trading the American Express form of consumption for the *La Bohème* kind? Not necessarily. Harvard Business School professor Teresa Amabile showed that it is possible to be a soulful striver: external rewards *can* support internal motivations as long as the rewards aren't valued in a competitive way. If the value of a reward is primarily the opportunity to do more and better work, then rewards don't hurt motivations. It's okay to yearn for that promotion, that grant, that raise, as long as the purpose isn't just racking up that stuff but of getting the chance to take meaningful action, devote extensive time to a challenging project, or what have you. As psychologist Richard O'Connor wrote in his recent book *Happy at Last: The Thinking Person's Guide to Finding Joy*, "In my experience with patients rich and poor, the really good things that money can get you are autonomy, security, and the time to enjoy life." Using material rewards in the service of internal goals is helpful.

Less helpful is using stuff as a way to make up for a lack of challenge, intimacy, meaning, or *fun* in life. Some people turn to materialism as a way of coping with self-image problems. Being aware of the discrepancy between what you know you are and what you wish you could be can be stressful—some folks like to deal with it by dressing the part. A pair of German psychologists discovered that the more nervous you make people about their identity, the more materialistic and status-oriented they become. Novice tennis players reminded of their lack of skill chose fancier brand-name equipment and clothing.*

Compensatory materialism can also be a lifelong coping mechanism against emotional or physical insecurity. Poverty can lead to materialistic values—poorer individuals become more materialistic, and entire nations develop more materialistic values during hard economic times. In countries where women have less access to education, public life, and birth control, they

---

* I wonder if hustlers—always several steps ahead of research psychologists—have figured out that the best marks are the folks sporting the shiniest, fanciest, least-used-looking equipment? Although when I phrase it like that, it's obvious they must have realized this ages ago.

are more likely to highly value money and status in a potential husband.

It doesn't even take long-term disenfranchisement and poverty to create materialistic values. Short-term anxiety—the kind social scientists can whip up in the lab, say, with a single sneer from an attractive research assistant—can also trigger compensatory materialism. After all, who hasn't succumbed to the urge to spiff up for a job interview or a high school reunion?

As the economic situation in America becomes increasingly insecure, it is reasonable to expect that some people will drift further down the path of materialism—as a psychological defense mechanism, a strategic choice to look the part they wish to play in life, or both—than they might have in more stable times. Those whose values are already pointed away from the material, in the meantime, will have a strong incentive to remain as they are. In other words, Phil, Mel, and Sam are likely to become even more set in their ways during hard times, and thereby find it even harder to maintain good relations.

If you're more like Freegan Phil . . .

Freegan Phils should keep in mind that Material Mel is not personally responsible for every starving orphan in Africa and Supersaver Sam isn't an interest-free bank.

You should be careful not to assume that your friends are delighted to subsidize your lifestyle. Refrain from hitting up friends for rides, bringing over music to play on a Material Mel's fine Bose CD player, and asking a Supersaver Sam to spot the cost of dinner. Your moral and money choices should primarily inconvenience *you.*

You should avoid invoking a holy string of "never's" and "always's" in describing material life, as they're sure to bite back (the way such statements often do). Someday, it may indeed be more satisfying to buy a DVD instead of waiting for its arrival at the public library. Besides, people are more likely to see the value in the way you live if it obviously makes you *happy*. Framing the issue as "I just like to keep things simple and make sure I've got money to spend on the things that are really important to me" is more attractive than "I don't want to contribute to corporate evil any more than I have to, you capitalist dog."

If you're more like Material Mel . . .

A Freegan Phil may not own a Lexus and a Supersaver Sam may have bought a factory-flawed suit at a bargain basement, but that doesn't make them losers or unappreciative of the finer things in life. Don't judge others for not having a new car or designer clothes and don't blame them for not being forced to buy those things in order to fit in at work or elsewhere.

If you believe you need to do certain things in order to maintain your professional edge—travel, grooming, socializing, continuing education—do them. No one else can really assess your situation and needs, so don't let a Freegan Phil or a Supersaver Sam draw you into an argument about the morality or responsibility of your spending. And don't you try to tempt them into one because you feel an itch to defend yourself.

Don't treat the Freegan Phils in your life as though they're quixotic dreamers out of touch with the real world. They're adults making informed choices, and there's just as much you don't know about their lives as they don't know about yours. Besides, if the economy collapses, a Freegan Phil will have the making-do skills to save your well-toned ass. (Until the apocalypse, though, don't rely on Phil's home-repair skills when you could just as easily learn to do it yourself or hire a professional. Freeloading on someone else's skills is just as tacky as freeloading on their money.)

If you're more like Supersaver Sam . . .

You could at least say that Freegan Phil and Material Mel are living the financial lives they desire. Supersaver Sams, on the third hand, are apt to invest so much moral meaning into being a "good money manager" that they feel a compulsion to save others from irresponsible, even childish, behavior. But it's best to keep the value judgments on hold, tend your own financial garden, and resist the temptation to weed those of others. Just as other people are allowed to have bad fashion sense, grammar, and posture without you correcting them, they're also allowed to be bad money managers.

You should think of your smart money management as a reward for yourself—and not as a skill you're developing for financial jousts with friends and family. Don't judge people by their credit scores—or deem someone as more or less "adult" based on their ability to acquire the props of adulthood, such as a house (also known as a mortgage).

Only give advice when you're asked to do so. Yes, it can be annoying to hear a Material Mel constantly whine about her credit card debt and then see her run off to the spa every weekend for seaweed wraps and hot stone massages, but it's not your problem to fix. Do you ever bemoan your waistline and then have another glass of wine? Wish you had more patience and then fail to meditate? Complain that your child doesn't pick up after himself—and then pick up after him? Of course you do. Humans are very good at complaining and very bad at resisting temptation and forming new habits. So cut others the slack you hope they will cut you and the ones you love. If you think you have never, ever complained about situations caused by your own behavior, think harder—or ask your close friends for an example. Trust me, they'll have one.

Social Credit

As much as we might want to get beyond materialism, a certain amount of consumption is required to be considered polite. How annoyed would you get at a friend who in this day and age did not have an answering machine or voice mail? Not to have voice mail seems ostentatiously rude, as though one were deliberately making inconveniences for others. Indeed, based on the view of Adam Smith, probably still the unrivaled expert on capitalism, voice mail is, in many respects, modern society's linen shirt:

> A linen shirt, for example, is strictly speaking, not a necessary of life. The Greeks and Romans lived, I suppose, very comfortably though they had no linen. But in the present times, though the greater part of Europe, a creditable day-labourer would be ashamed to appear in public without a linen shirt, the want of which would be supposed to denote that disgraceful degree of poverty which, it is presumed, nobody can fall into without extreme bad conduct.

But beyond the answering machine, "excessive" consumption is to a large extent in the eye of the beholder. Juliet Schor, the well-known critic of consumer culture, notes that much of the overspending in America is defensive in character—not the expression of spoiled entitlement as much as it is fear of falling behind.

Decisions about consumption aren't made in a vacuum but in the context of other people's choices. It's not just a matter of ego or evolutionary holdovers that makes us want to keep up with the Joneses, either: there are real social and economic costs to not having the right appearance, credentials, manners, knowledge, or accent. As economist Robert H. Frank notes: "When those at the top spend more on interview suits, others just below them must spend more as well, or else face lower odds of being hired. When upper-middle-class professionals buy six-thousand-pound Range Rovers, others with lower incomes must buy heavier vehicles as well, or else face greater risks of dying."

In an increasingly competitive, no-guarantees economy, this sort of spending—however difficult to justify in terms of morality or even desire—may seem increasingly necessary. Economists have been writing about the "beauty premium" for over a decade now—the fact that good looks have a real impact on a person's economic future. Good looks, of course, can to some extent be bought. And who's to blame the individual who decides to give him- or herself such an edge? (That "him-" isn't just a nod to political correctness; the beauty premium applies to men, too.) As Frank points out, one of the aspects of a fast-moving business world is that we must often make quick decisions about people under conditions of some uncertainty. When we have to make quick decisions, appearances play a huge part in our reasoning. Therefore, Frank reasons, "To the extent that wearing the right watch, driving the right car, wearing the right suit, or living in the right neighborhood might help someone land the right job or a big contract, these expenditures are more like investments than true consumption." Supersaver Sam has real reason to spend so much time and mental energy on finding the "highest-return" suit for her budget.

According to sociologist Juliet Schor, we no longer strive simply to keep up with the Joneses in the house or office next door, whom we may know primarily for the intricacy of their landscaping or the size of their expense account. Our socioeconomic "reference group" is now those people—real ones and the media's representations—who are vaguely "like us" in terms of careers, politics, taste, and consumer choices. These are the people from whom we inherit our material taste. As an example, Schor notes how "poet-waiters earning $18,000 a year, teachers earning $30,000, and editors and publishers earning six-figure incomes all aspire to be part of one urban literary reference group." In some cases (the real-life ones), these people may have attended the same schools or met at the same first jobs, but over the subsequent five to twenty years they've landed in significantly different money situations. Learning how to be comfortable with friends, acquaintances, and colleagues hailing from different income bands—and handling the economic turns of fortune in their lives—is a crucial social skill.

Rich Friend, Poor Friend

Let's say Penny decided to take her liberal-arts degree and go work for a nonprofit, and her college roommate and best friend Millicent went on to business school and is now a pricey investment counselor. Can this friendship be saved? Of course it can. But first, both Penny and Millicent must choose to be unembarrassed by their different circumstances. Millicent isn't more successful than Penny; she just has more money. Penny isn't more virtuous than Millicent; she just has less money. If Penny hates her landlord and her ten-year-old car, it isn't Millicent's fault. If Millicent hates her long work hours, it isn't Penny's fault. Take the symbolic element—the status—away from the money, and it becomes as morally neutral as the fact that Penny has blue eyes and Millicent brown.

Penny should feel comfortable suggesting restaurants and activities that she can afford. But she should also not stand all "po'-but-proud" when Millicent offers to buy her a fancy dinner or baseball tickets. (An obviously status-conscious gift would be opera tickets, but in Boston, at least, you can hear decent opera for much less than you'd pay for good seats at a Sox game. Certain things carry the whiff of elitism about them regardless of actual cost; "sipping chardonnay" is practically code for "out-of-touch elitist," but a bottle of Two-Buck Chuck isn't going to set you back any more than a six-pack of Miller Lite would.) Of course, if Millicent picked up the tab all the time, that would risk putting Penny on the level of a paid companion, rewarded for her amusing chatter with Grey Goose martinis and steak frites, and eventually the friendship would start to wear as both women started to feel a bit taken advantage of. But the occasional splurge is perfectly all right.

How to be a good poor friend

If you're the church mouse in your circle of friends, don't think that your modest circumstances buy you out of your social obligations.

- **Give gifts,** even if all you can afford is homemade cookies or a box of nice stationery.

- **Entertain,** even if your home and accoutrements don't measure up to those of others. Mostly, people delight in seeing friends and breaking routine, and in getting out of the house and enjoying nice conversation and maybe some food. If the only kinds of parties you can afford to throw are potlucks and BYOBs, throw potlucks and BYOBs. If everyone else in your circle can afford better, then you've got novelty value on your side, which isn't an advantage to be discounted.

• **Don't hold your friends' money against them.** It can be easy to slide into resentment of people who have more money than you do, even if you love them dearly. Keep in mind that you may not have the full story: a richer friend may be riddled with debt in a way you can't imagine, or be golden-handcuffed to a job she hates, or be supporting an aged parent in an expensive care facility. And you might not know what her money means to her: she might have grown up with such financial insecurity that no amount of money will make her feel safe, or she may be comparing herself to someone other than you—the richest person in your circle might be the poorest person in her family.

• **Don't expect to be paid for.** Don't feel as though your richer friend owes you anything. If he wants to pop for dinner occasionally, say thank you and don't feel obligated to reciprocate beyond your budget. If he doesn't, don't begrudge him for it. All friends owe one another respect and consideration, but if you feel angry, embarrassed, or ashamed about your financial position, that is *your* problem to work through, no one else's. Get as comfortable saying, "Oh, let's not go out to eat. I'm on a budget this week," as you are saying, "Let's not go out tonight, I have a cold coming on." It's nicer to have money and no cold, but if that isn't your situation, there's no shame in it. Neither says anything about your worth as a person—and your friends *know that*.

✦ I can afford good food and booze these days, but affording a decent house to entertain *in* is another matter entirely. We have a very odd apartment setup, with the kitchen in the attic (sans microwave, sans dishwasher, sans ice maker, sans cabinets—sans everything) and a dining room downstairs, which rather puts a cramp in my style. I can't make the nice dinners that are so easy for our friends, what with their "work islands" and matching glassware and fancy-schmancy stoves where all the burners light.

For a while I let that intimidate and shame me out of entertaining, and our social obligations started to pile up like dirty dishes. Then one magical day it hit me that our friends like *us*, and their enjoyment of our company isn't mitigated by the presence of plastic forks. So until I have a dishwasher, I'm using paper plates and plastic cups when I entertain. Until I have a kitchen and dining room on the same floor, I'm cooking one-pot meals or ordering out. A recent innovation has been "pizza and cheap champagne" nights, where we have four to eight folks over and get—you guessed it—pizza and cheap champagne. It's terrific fun! We put a lot of thought into the guest list, and not much at all into anything else. Our friends enjoy it, and you know damn well they're not going to worry, the next time they want to see us, that the bathroom still hasn't been renovated or that chicken Marbella is too clichéd. By freeing yourself up to live comfortably with your imperfections, you liberate others to do the same.

How to be a good rich friend

What's the opposite of a church mouse—a bank mouse? If you're the bank mouse, don't be embarrassed about your money, but do be mindful of how your circumstances affect your social life.

- **Keep in mind what your friends can afford.** If you want to go somewhere more expensive than your friends can afford, offer to pay, but remember you're not doing your friends a life-changing favor, you're just shelling out a bit extra for the pleasure of their company by candlelight (or footlights, or the glare of Fenway Park). Make it clear *up front* when something is going to be on your dime: "Let's have dinner at Chez Fancypants, my treat" or "I want to take you to Chez Fancypants for your birthday" is the way to do it. Otherwise you're on a likely collision for that horribly awkward moment where you ask someone out assuming it will be your treat, and then they say it's out of their budget, and then you make it clear that you intended to pay, which makes it sound like you weren't going to until you found out they were poor. And all you'll succeed in doing at that point is making your friend feel like an object of charity rather than a celebrant.

- **Entertain.** If you're entertaining at home, do it up as big as you like; you're not showing off, you're showing folks a good time. (I have pizza and cheap champagne at *my* underamenitied house; when I'm hanging with monied friends, I'd like them to fire up all four burners on that Aga and make me something *fancy* while I drink their good single malt.) Pretending to have less than you do is no more attractive than pretending to have more than you do.

• **Don't expect to pay.** If your poorer friend suggests somewhere pricier than usual, don't counter by suggesting Chang's Cheap Chinese; your friend knows what he can afford and what he can't. It's insulting to imply that not only is he poor, he's also too stupid to know it.

Allow your poorer friends to pick up the tab, occasionally; if you don't, they'll feel like you're treating them like children. This can be a sore point for poorer friends. Often it's not that they feel unsuccessful or deprived; they feel as though they're not quite grown up, a natural and uncomfortable feeling in a society that readily equates being an adult with professional success and money. Be sensitive to this when you're dealing with friends who have less money than you, especially if they are a bit younger. (If they're *really* younger it doesn't matter, because then they'll figure that when they're old like you, they'll be rich, too. It's the five-to-fifteen-year age gap that you have to watch out for.)

• **Don't hold your friends' lack of money against them.** Don't feel shy mentioning your travels or your art collection or your fantastic Bose sound system if it comes up in conversation; if you aggressively steer the talk away from it, you might leave your friends suspecting you don't want to stoke their jealousy—not a winning strategy. (Of course, anyone who harps on his cool stuff all the time quickly becomes a bore, even to people who have equally cool stuff themselves.)

If a poorer friend has an attitude problem about your money or her lack thereof, it is her problem, not yours. If she tells you she can't afford to do something or calls you out on some clueless statement of privilege, that's one thing; snarky comments about how it "must be nice" or "it's not like you'd know" are another. You can respond with, "It sounds as though you're angry with me for some reason," or, if the situation requires you to be more direct, try, "When you say that it makes me feel that you resent me for having money." Adding "I can't help that" is a good way of defusing the situation. It protects you from falling into the treacherous line of defense, "I worked hard for that money," which implies that your friend has less money because she is either lazy or stupid for not choosing a more remunerative field. And don't try to ameliorate the situation by sharing your own financial woes. Moaning "I took *such* a hit on capital-gains taxes this year" probably won't endear you to someone who doesn't have health insurance.

• **Think before offering financial assistance.** The minute a poorer friend mentions, say, a medical or credit card bill that's looming large in his budget but would be little or no problem for you, don't leap to say, "Hey, let me take care of that for you." Take a day or two—even if you knew instantly that you want to help—so that your friend will know you really mean it. As with all favors, financial and non-, let the friend know that he will be doing a kindness to *you* to allow you to give without getting in return.

The Trick behind the Perfect Gift

A whole book could be written about gift giving, from gift picking to regifting to unwanted gifts to wedding gifts to baby shower gifts to thank-you notes, and I'll probably write one someday. For now, I'll forgo details and focus on the basic principles of gift giving, particularly giving monetary gifts.

Except at showers and similar functions, the purpose of gift giving isn't primarily to bestow yet more material *stuff* upon people but rather to express our affection for and knowledge of them. The "affection and knowledge" thing is still important at baby and wedding showers. But gifts for these events are primarily intended to set up a new household or member thereof and are thus somewhat more utilitarian than expressive. While giving money seems to avoid many of the pitfalls of gift giving and receiving—wrong size, wrong color, wrong taste, wrong *everything*—it conveys that you do not know the recipient well enough to choose an appropriate gift. (Unless, that is, you know they—and it's usually "they"—are saving for a major purchase, such as a house or a honeymoon.) If you really don't know the recipient(s) that well—you want to give something to the grown child of an old family friend who lives out of town, say—that's fine. But the message can be an insulting one to send to people whose tastes you do, or at least *should*, know.

The fact that money as a gift means "I can't figure you out" does, however, make it the ideal option for children, teenagers, and college-aged adults, who take it as the highest compliment to be considered unreadable by their elders. If you suspect that the young'uns are likely to fritter away the cash on pizza or parking tickets or laundry (or slot) machines, and won't buy something substantial like you want them to, give them a gift certificate instead. Just make sure it's to a store (or movie theater or restaurant) that they do or would frequent and that exists in their neighborhood. You'd be surprised—at least I have been—by how many well-meaning gift card bestowers don't do that basic research.

Giving charitable donations in the recipient's name is also a nice thing, if you do it right. If you choose to give charitable donations in lieu of gifts, make sure that the donations are to causes that are either wholly innocuous and nonpolitical or reflect the recipient's values. It's annoying to have money given in your name to an organization you disagree with, and even worse when you remain on their mailing list for years to come.

While there's no reason ever to give your money to an organization whose goals you disagree with, the gift of a charitable contribution should reflect the values and priorities of the person in whose name it is given, not the person who put up the cash. Your favorite cause may be hot meals for the housebound, but you should donate to, say, animal welfare in the name of your friend who graduated from veterinary school, or to cancer research for the coworker who lost her father to leukemia, or to childhood literacy for the neighbor who is retiring after thirty years as a kindergarten teacher. And don't make a donation you'd make anyway and just stick someone else's name on it and make a "gift" out of it. Regifting is acceptable, within limits, but moral double dipping is not. If you want to make a charitable donation in someone else's name but keep them from getting endless follow-up mailings, you can contact the organization and ask them to send donation cards and envelopes to you. When the cards arrive, write your message on the donation card and send it to your recipients. This way you receive the tax credit for the donation and your recipients retain their privacy.

If you're solicited for charity, at your workplace or anywhere else, you don't have to give if you can't afford it, and you shouldn't feel a social obligation to give to a cause you don't support. Explain nicely that you've already spent your charity budget for the given year, or that you prefer to give larger amounts to a smaller number of groups. Any solicitation at work most definitely ought to be for causes that anyone could support—no one, presumably, is *for* leukemia or childhood illiteracy—and not for potentially controversial political or religious groups (if you are asked to contribute to such a group, alert HR or the boss). If workplace solicitation is done in a public fashion—sign-up sheets outside someone's office door to support her in a Walk for Good Things, say—bring it up with the boss. This kind of social pressure isn't appropriate and can undermine office morale.

The Trick behind Splitting the Bill

There are lots of ways to divide a restaurant tab fairly: trying to figure out who owes what, requesting separate checks, taking turns picking up the tab, splitting it down the middle.

1. The "who owes what" method seems to be the most common but also certainly the least efficient—my husband has a math degree from Harvard and I've been out plenty of times with him and a group of high-powered scientists, and *still* no one can figure out the check. It's even worse when everyone has "ATM disease"—nothing but twenties in their wallets.

2. Separate checks are a good idea, but be mindful and ask for them in advance. Otherwise it's a big pain for the servers.

3. Taking turns paying is congenial, and in fact behavioral economist Dan Ariely of Duke University has determined that this is the most pleasure-maximizing way of handling the situation, since both giving to others and receiving a "present" are enjoyable experiences.* This practice works best, though, if you frequently go out with the same people, if everyone in the group makes more or less the same amount of money, if you usually go to restaurants in similar price ranges, and if you're organized enough to remember who paid last time. That's a slew of conditions. Plus, if there's a "social director" who usually drives, finds the night when everyone can get together, asks her babysitter to watch your kid as well, or makes the reservations, that person should get dinner bought for her once in a while, by way of a thank-you.

4. Splitting down the middle works when everyone usually eats and drinks the same amount. Drinkers should generally pay more (but, of course, they've been drinking, so the nondrinkers might need to remind them of that). If tab splitting seems to be working to your disadvantage more often than not, switch to getting separate checks. Tell your friends that it's for "budgeting" or "bookkeeping" reasons, a vague excuse that people almost always go along with, rather than pointing out to them that their gluttony is costing you money.

---

* Dan Ariely won the 2008 Ig Nobel medicine prize, along with colleagues Rebecca L. Waber, Baba Shiv, and Ziv Carmon, for demonstrating that high-priced placebos are more effective than low-priced placebos.

And then there's the situation when someone goes for the check. Let them, unless you have a compelling business reason to insist on paying for the meal, for example, because there's a company policy that clients don't pay or you're hosting a potential job candidate. I'm a big believer that the correct reply to "Let me get this" is "Thank you." No one should have to argue for the right to buy you dinner—or lunch, for that matter. And if he didn't really mean it and expected you to demur—well, he'll know better the time after that.

I say "the time after that" because, of course, you'll be picking up the next tab.

· 3 ·

Happy Holidays

RELIGION

"My ancestors were Puritans from England. They
arrived here in 1648 in the hope of finding greater
restrictions than were permissible under English law
at that time."

—Garrison Keillor

The diversity of American religious experience, combined with how very seriously we take religion as a
country, is impressive. Uptight Puritans' blue laws against alcohol sales on Sundays still exist in parts of America, right along-
side "Kumbaya," the stirring and unifying multidenominational
anthem that was exported to Africa by Christian missionaries
before being reimported to the New Age 1960s. Some Muslim
women honor the *hijab* by donning jeans and a head scarf, while
others choose to wear burkas. And in Brooklyn, New York, Ha-
sidic Jews celebrating Sukkoth offer greetings of joy to their
Rastafarian neighbors. Happy holidays, indeed.

Religion is found in all cultures, and our exposure to a mul-
titude of religious beliefs and behavior has only grown over the
past century. In the United States, which according to Andrew
Kohut of the Pew Research Center is alternately viewed by both
Americans and the rest of the world as too religious and not

religious enough, this increasing diversity plays out in some un- expected ways. But first, let's get a better handle on the universal qualities of religion. Then, we'll get into tips for behaving gra- ciously when people express their religious belief in ways differ- ent from yourself. After service, we'll all meet back in the social hall for coffee and bagels.

Why Religion Is All Over the Place (Literally)

Religion is considered to be a universal that exists across cultures. But it's only been in the past decade or so that we've begun to have the slightest idea of why that is. For the longest time—with the exception of William James's *Varieties of Religious Experience* (a book more often praised than actually read)—the psychology of religion was dominated by Freudians, neo-Freudians, post- Freudians, and contra-Freudians, all of whose basic idea was that whatever issues you had with Daddy down here on earth, you just projected onto Daddy in the Big Sky.* With the dual advent of brain imaging and evolutionary psychology, however, the ques- tion of religion got to be quite the hot topic indeed. Suddenly we had new ways of explaining what attracted people to religion. And events like the blowing up of abortion clinics and Buddha statues and Twin Towers suggest we might want to fine-tune those explanations sooner rather than later. People couldn't be all *that* angry with their daddies.

Contemporary psychology suggests three main reasons for religion: 1) it's good for us, 2) our brains are wired that way, part one, and 3) our brains are wired that way, part two. Now,

---

* It was a little more nuanced than that, but I've never felt a strong compulsion to play fair with psychoanalysts.

none of these addresses the ultimate truth of any religion or the existence of God, so I'm going to lay out some guidelines for how I'll be talking about religion, and religious courtesy, in this chapter.

Looking at the naturalistic basis of a phenomenon doesn't mean there is no transcendent aspect to it. There's a biological basis for my attraction to Mr. Improbable, and a neurochemical description of what goes on in my brain when he does something improbably adorable, but that doesn't mean I'm not really in love with him. So it is, too, with religion. If you're a religious person, imagine that tingling sensation of first falling in love and then read the next couple pages to appreciate your faith, and human religious belief, in a whole new way.

Religion is good for us

The findings on the effects of religion on individuals' well-being are mixed. If religion helps you avoid intoxicants, spend time each day in silent contemplation, or find a supportive group of people who bring you casseroles or a slaughtered goat or whatever is culturally appropriate when you're ill—then sure, you're going to benefit. On the other hand, if religion leads you to starve yourself to support the priestly class, abuse your children in the name of righteousness, or quarantine yourself when ill because you've displeased the gods, then chances are it's going to ratchet up the "nasty, brutish, and short" component of life. In the United States today, where member-hungry churches offer Starbucks in the lobbies, bowling nights, and Christian aerobics, religion seems to make people pretty happy: people who go to church report more life satisfaction than those who don't, and religious folks often test out a little happier than nonreligious ones. Historically speaking, though, it's pretty much been a coin toss. Hot dishes or battered children, cake or death. So much for religion improving individual fitness.

Some scholars focus not so much on religion's effect on the *individual* but on the *group*. Religious groups behave better toward one another, the theory goes, because there are rules to follow, with God or the spirits or the principle of karma always watching (over) you. In the jargon of the field, religion encourages pro-social behavior and discourages social cheating (attempting to get one's own back scratched more than one intends to scratch others' in return). This is a stronger argument than the idea that it's good for us individually.

Granted, other animals seem to get along in groups pretty well without having religion. As Frans de Waal recounts in *Peacemaking among Primates,* nonhuman primates have created some fairly effective manners of their own for keeping flat-out competition and aggression in check. (It's the book in which de Waal launched the bonobos' slogan "Make love, not war" to describe the species' prolific use of sex to relieve social tension.) But then, other animals also haven't evolved the capacity to *lie.* Once you can lie—once you can hurt and cheat people, to their faces, in a way they can't immediately detect—the idea that God is always watching is a pretty effective way to keep people in line. Just read the Hebrew Bible: immense chunks of Genesis and Exodus are all about people trying to live peaceably in groups, messing it up by lying to one another, and dragging God in to sort things out.

"Good for the group" is one possible reason that religion pops up everywhere and sticks around much longer than social scientists posit it ought to. And that's exactly where some of our contemporary problems come in—religion is good for the *tribe*. And unless you're Amish or FLDS or otherwise living in some theological enclave (in which case, I hope for your sake that you've upholstered this book in gingham and hidden it under your mattress), a lot of your dealings are going to be with the unsaved, the unenlightened, the *goyim*, the *dhimmis*, the *harbis*—whatever unflattering term your particular religion uses to describe nonmembers. (Or the Jesus freaks, God-botherers, fundamorons, fanatics, or whatever unflattering terms your *non*religion uses to describe nonmembers.) Our "good for the group" mentality needs to be expanded beyond its original scope if we're going to live together gracefully.

Our brains are wired for religion, part one

The argument that we've evolved to believe involves research in a field called "neurotheology," a word that, if you're feeling conversationally frisky, you can toss out at your next cocktail party, seder, or barn raising. Neurotheology is the idea that the brain is structured in a certain way—it's not just sloshing around in there like so much clever yogurt, after all—and when that structure gets lit up in a certain way, when the right weather system is blowing over the terrain, humans have religious experiences. Feelings of oneness, awe, boundless love, awareness of the infinite, and so on. The fun bit is that no one seems to be able to agree what that particular lighting pattern looks like. Cognitive neuroscientist Michael Persinger, who uses an apparatus called a "god helmet" to replicate religious experiences, thinks that they have something to do with the relationship between the left and right hemispheres of the brain. Doctors Andrew Newberg and Eugene D'Aquili, the authors of *Why God Won't Go Away: Brain Science and the Bi-*

ology of Belief, believe religious epiphanies are tied to moments when the parietal lobe quiets down. V. S. Ramachandran, the "Marco Polo of neuroscience," fingers the left temporal lobe, and the author of *Zen and the Brain: Toward an Understanding of Meditation and Consciousness*, James H. Austin, suggests that a pruning of the neurons in the cortex and limbic system can be spiritually helpful.*

The most plausible conclusion to draw from all of this is that *something* happens *somewhere* in the brain during at least *some* kinds of religious experiences—which should hardly surprise anyone. Neurotheological experiments are full of all kinds of pitfalls. One of the reasons that religion is so powerful is the range of experiences it offers, from mystical ecstasy to text study to serving soup to the homeless to creating or appreciating great works of music and architecture, and trying to find "the religion center" in your brain is kind of like trying to find "the store" in a megamall. And since almost any experience labeled "religious" can also be experienced in a nonreligious context—atheists are just as capable of mysticism, scholasticism, altruism, and aesthetics as their religious brethren—it's difficult to know if it's really a "religious" experience that is being measured. Most neurotheology studies are conducted using functional magnetic resonance imaging (fMRI) machines, which are claustrophobic and loud— about a hundred decibels, or as loud as a chain saw, motorcycle, or the worst of the New York City subways. Anyone who could achieve satori in Times Square would certainly be worth studying,

---

* You could read a bunch of actual journal articles about this, like I did. Or for a more reader-friendly journey into the "God lives 'ere in the brain! Nao 'e doesn't, 'e's over 'ere, ye great stupid git!" debate, check out John Horgan's *Rational Mysticism: Dispatches from the Border Between Science and Spirituality*.

but I'm not sure many universal conclusions could be drawn from her experience. Neurotheology may be helpful for differentiating between types of religious/spiritual experiences, but it doesn't seem likely to give us the answer for why religion is so universal.

Our brains are wired for religion, part two

The most fashionable and inclusive explanation for religion these days comes out of cognitive-evolutionary psychology— the branch of psychology that's all about why we think the way we think. Why *do* we think the way we think? Because those habits of mind helped us survive back in the harsh and unforgiving days of our species' youth.

For example, the human mind seems predisposed to notice patterns. This is a good thing, generally. If you learn to notice the signs for an impending storm, you can get in your cave before it hits. Learn to notice the shifty-eyed glance Og makes before he tries to put one over on you, and you'll watch him more carefully the next time the tribe is dividing up the mammoth. Pattern recognition is so useful to us that we'll see patterns in everything, including random coincidences. And we're not the only animals who do this—pretty much any animal intelligent enough to learn (which is all of them, as long as you don't have very high expectations of *what* they can learn) will recognize patterns, because linking your own behavior to an outcome is pattern recognition. In 1948, B. F. Skinner put pigeons in a box installed with a timer that, at regular intervals, released feed to the birds. Sure enough, the pigeons quickly decided that whatever they'd been doing before the manna came down—pecking, scratching, doing a little pigeon dance—had caused the goodies to flow. So they'd keep doing it, just like a ballplayer will decide that the tightie-whiteys he wore during a no-hitter are his "lucky underwear" and wear them for every major game. (Research shows that people who are more than usually prone to see patterns—in strings of random numbers, say—are more likely to believe in superstitions and psychic phenomena.) Many religious rituals probably developed in a similar fashion. I've always found it amusing that in the Jewish liturgical calendar, the prayer for rain comes in early December—right before rainy season in Israel.

Unlike other animals, as far as we know, humans also tend to assume that events *mean* something, and that figuring out what they mean is the key to responding appropriately. Particularly crucial: figuring out the intentions of others. Is Oonah really too sick to go out grub gathering or is she faking it so that she can get grubs without doing any work? Is that tribe on the other side of the hills holding out their stone knives because they want to trade them for our furs, or are they indicating they will kill us if we enter their territory? Get these answers wrong—or, worse yet, fail to recognize even the existence of the questions—and you're not around for very long. Because detecting intentions, like recognizing patterns, was key for our survival, it's not shocking that we developed, or overdeveloped, "intention detectors." We started to think, consciously or not, that there must be some intentional mind behind natural events just as there is behind social events. Infertility and illness are signs of the gods' displeasure, good weather and game a sign of their delight.*

The fact that religion appears to have natural origins based in our evolution and reflected in our brain chemistry says nothing about the ultimate truth of religious beliefs or experiences.

---

* Sure, nonbelievers, have a good laugh—because *you've* never said, "This computer hates me," right?

What is important is that, taken together, these data and theories seem to suggest that our brains and societies were primed for religion long before the recorded history of any particular known sect.

They also suggest that even in nonreligious societies, religious-like behaviors will persist. Massachusetts is one of the most unbelieving states in the nation, according to a recent Pew Research Center poll, but if Red Sox Nation isn't a quasi religion, I don't know what is. I was teaching at a Catholic school in Boston when the Sox broke the curse in 2004, as well as when John Paul II died and Pope Benedict was installed in 2005. While one can never know what lies in the heart of another, my strong impression is that more frequent and fervent prayers were made in that school in 2004.

Why Religion Is All Over the Place (Metaphorically)

"The religious life of the American people may not yet have experienced the turbulence of professional sports, where free agents search around for the team that will offer them the best contract. . . . But it does seem to be heading in that direction."
—Alan Wolfe, The Transformation of American Religion

While religious behaviors and beliefs may be universal across cultures, they come in an astonishingly wide variety across individuals. Religion offers unparalleled "one-stop shopping" for a variety of human needs. Joining a worship community gives you an instant family of people who speak the same language, know the same stories, hold the same values, and will help you when you need it. The benefits of this kind of instant community in an increasingly mobile society are obvious. Churches and other religious organizations can provide leadership opportunities to people who might not get such opportunities in their professional lives—maybe you're just a receptionist at work, but at church you can be a teacher, an organizer, a mentor, a counselor. If you are inclined toward mystical experiences, your tradition can help you learn to pray or meditate. If you are more interested in the outside world than in the inner landscape, you can work on a social justice, charity, or political initiative. If you are moved by art or literature, you can study the great works of your tradition and even try your hand at creating your own—poetry, painting, fiber arts, music, calligraphy. You can study the original language of your faith, or teach it. Emotional support, practical help, networking and professional development, spiritual growth, political empowerment, aesthetic appreciation, continuing education: religions offer *all* of these, and they offer them to *everyone* who belongs. I can't think of any other human institution that offers such a wide range of benefits to its members.

Of course, not everyone is going to take advantage of every single benefit. Some people like to serve soup to the homeless, others like to explicate texts, others prefer silent contemplation of the divine. People's "tastes" in religious experiences are not unlike their different preferences for food. Some part of the difference is probably based in biology.* Biologically, however, we also each carry a set of psychological temperaments and,

---

* The entertainingly contradictory nature of the neurotheology research may simply have to do with the different ways people can have religious experiences. Scientists used to believe that different tastes were perceived in different parts of the tongue—the "tongue map" you may have learned in school, in which the tip of the tongue tasted sweets, the back tasted bitters, and so on. The thing is, as was discovered all the way back in 1974, that tongue map is bunk; we taste flavors all over the tongue. Still, who knows: maybe there's a "spirituality map" in the brain somewhere, sampling the sweet, salty, sour, and bitter flavors of faiths.

sometimes, needs. Like with our food preferences, our religious preferences are set by our individual and family backgrounds—the positive (and negative) interactions we have with religious belief over the course of our lives. A major factor is finding a community in which we feel comfortable, people who feel "like us" in some ineffable way. The flexibility and power of religious tradition lie in its ability to meet those diverse needs at the local level.

America's separation of church and state, by refusing to privilege any one religion, has opened the door for religions to compete for as many community members as they can attract. Over the past several decades, that's led to a sort of marketplace mentality and a churning around of religious identities. According to Alan Wolfe in *The Transformation of American Religion: How We Actually Live Our Faith*, a 1955 Gallup Poll reported that only 4 percent of Americans had switched from the religious denominations into which they were born; a Pew poll in 2008, by contrast, showed that 44 percent had.

The Sacred and the Bazaar

"Just as the political differences among states are not as great as the political differences among communities, the greatest political disparities are among individual churches, not denominations. Forget whether the church is Baptist or Episcopalian. The important question is whether the service begins with praise music, Handel, or Sting."

—Bill Bishop, *The Big Sort*

The American marketplace of religions is as chock full of choices as our supermarkets. Today, people are looking, to an unprecedented degree, at options not only within their own tradition ("Should I join the bowling league or the hospital-visitation group?") but across many religious traditions ("Should I be a Methodist or a Buddhist—or both?"). Americans are devout but not self-abnegating—we won't go to a church that doesn't meet our needs.

Alan Wolfe draws an interesting parallel between trends in religion and the workplace: "America will no longer be the 'denominational society' for the same reason that its (male) workers will no longer be 'organization men.'" Increasingly, when thinking about their professional and religious lives, Americans don't ask themselves, "What organization should I be with?" but rather "What do I believe in, what am I good at, what kinds of people do I like to be with?" and then find a workplace—or a church—that matches their skills, values, and needs. If the organization stops working out, you make a change; people no longer feel that they've abandoned their faith by leaving one church for another any more than they feel they've ended their career when they quit their job.

With so much personal exploration of religion, we get, as a secondary benefit, a whole lot of acceptance for other religions, too. Wolfe's research uncovered that even evangelical Christians tend not to want to judge other religions harshly, and a 2008 Pew Forum poll showed that 70 percent of all religious people, and 57 percent of evangelical Christians, believe that other religions besides their own can lead to God. In the words of Public Agenda's report "For Goodness' Sake: Why So Many Want Religion to Play a Greater Role in American Life," "This is what ordinary Americans appear to ask of themselves: to walk a fine line, be true and represent your beliefs to the world, but do so in a way that does not judge or offend others."

Where the tolerance seems to end, however, is at the border

between the religious and the nonreligious. Fewer people report being willing to vote for an atheist than for a black person, a woman, a Jew, or a homosexual. This is a big cultural divide, the Grand Canyon of religious differences. Americans understand freedom of religion; when they're asked for freedom *from* religion, on the other hand, the religious all too often feel oppressed, a reaction that is incomprehensible to the nonreligious.

Evangelical Christians, in particular, are likely to feel impinged upon and to draw rather dramatic conclusions about their feelings: a recent poll reported that "84 percent of evangelicals agree that Satan is behind the fight against religion in public life in this country." A majority of evangelicals believe that they are the victims of media bias and prejudice. The distance between someone who feels like a victim and someone who doesn't believe at all is probably one that can't be breached. I should know—I've been on both sides.

Although I'm now a Reform Jew, I was raised as a fundamentalist Christian. I remember the feeling that the world was mocking us and all we held sacred. I remember the frustration when secular people told me that "because the Bible says so" wasn't a good enough answer. I remember the weird feeling of pleasure plus pain of being both persecuted and special, beloved by God and despised by the world. Those feelings are more powerful than any empirical logic or evidence in the world; you'll never win an argument against them.

But there can be common ground between religious and nonreligious folk, even between straight-up atheists and evangelicals. What most religious people in the United States are concerned with isn't doctrinal hairsplitting (we're actually pretty bad on doctrine, which I'll get to later) but morality. Poll after poll shows that damned near everyone in America these days is freaked out about the "decline of culture," the seemingly endless stream of rude drivers, political sex scandals, Internet porn, overconsumption—the things that make us feel we're losing our greatness as a nation, our warmth and connection as neighbors, and our capacity for joy and civility as individuals. I won't lie to you: no one really knows the fix. But religious people are likely to believe that more religion would help. According to a 2008 Public Agenda poll, religious people believe that if there was more religion, there would also be less crime, more volunteerism, less greed and materialism, and that people would do a better job raising their kids. Who wouldn't like to see those trends come to pass? In many ways, religious and nonreligious people want the same things for America; they just see different paths to getting there. Let's try to find some common ground.

Bless Who?

Question: *What is the proper response when a stranger, coworker, or acquaintance near me sneezes? Is it okay to say "Bless you" even if I don't know that person's religious preference? What if I offend an atheist by trying to be polite?*

The first thing that both religious and nonreligious people owe one another is to be good advertisements for their beliefs. Jewish tradition has a term—*chillul Hashem*—which means "desecration of God's name." This refers to anything that a Jew does that brings disgrace upon God, the Torah, or Jewish law. More liberal Jews also use it to refer to actions that disgrace the Jewish people and our values. The opposite of *chillul Hashem* is *kiddush Hashem*—to sanctify or bring glory to God.

This is a good concept for people of any religion or nonreligion to keep in mind—don't be the kind of person who gives members of your group a bad name. It's hard not to feel sorry for atheists these days. Atheism is a respectable and logical philosophical stance, and atheists deserve better than that misogynist lout Christopher Hitchens as their public face.* All of us should aim to avoid becoming the Hitch of our worldview.

Whether you're a believer or not

- **Be human, not divine.** For believers, this doesn't mean you have to act superbly pious every living minute. It's just not possible to be terribly, terribly joyful about your relationship with Jesus or Allah or the Eightfold Path all the time—believe me, people outside your religion, and quite possibly some of the more astute ones within it, see right through that act and pity you for it. For both believers and nonbelievers, admit your doubts when you have them— it makes your faith, or your lack thereof, all the more impressive.

- **Be a good neighbor.** The great nineteenth-century rabbi Yisrael Salantner once noted, "It is usual for a people to express concern for their own body and for their neighbor's soul. They seldom worry about their own soul and the other's body." He urged a reversal of these priorities, suggesting that a more appropriate state of mind would be concern with our own spiritual well-being and our

---

* Mindful manners don't require checking your opinions at the door.

neighbor's physical health and welfare. Not a bad way of looking at things.

How to be a believer around nonbelievers

• **Don't act as though your religion is an allergen.** When it comes to allergic atheists, it's gracious to be concerned about their feelings, especially since many people these days seem to assume atheists don't have feelings at all, but you're on safe ground saying "Bless you" when a person sneezes. The phrase doesn't state whose (or Whose) blessing is being invoked, after all. The sneezer is at perfect liberty to imagine that they are being blessed by Jesus, Krishna, Buddha, or, for that matter, by you, since you're the one who said it. Avoiding "God bless you" is generally wise, even when you're blessing someone you know believes in God. That phrase can just as easily prick the conscience of believers, who might feel you are taking the Lord's name in vain. If all these theological subtleties are enough to make you stick with "Gesundheit," I can't blame you a bit.

Contrary to myth, most atheists, agnostics, and plain old apathists are not horribly offended by religious language or imagery. (Some are, but the "mind over manners" credo says that we don't worry about folks who freak out over other people quietly doing their own thing.) In general, most nonbelievers aren't going to have a conniption over your crucifix, Sikh turban, bindi dot, or occasional reference to your spiritual practice. After all, they handle money every day with "In God We Trust" printed on it and don't break out in a rash. So don't censor yourself or become rabidly self-conscious.

• **Don't act as though your religion is an addiction.**
Believers needn't bring their religious preferences into
every single interaction. I mean, fine, if you think that's
what God wants you to do, you're going to do it anyway,
regardless of what I say. But the most likely effect it will
have on your fellow humans is to irritate them and make
them consider you predictable beyond all measure—a
judgment that quickly leads to people tuning you out
entirely.* Chronic God-talk will also make them wonder
if, deep down, you're really trying to convince *yourself*
(which, I assume, is the exact opposite of what you're
trying to achieve). Not only do people who engage in such
an extensive level of God-talk risk alienating nonbelieving
friends, but even the more spiritually minded can be
offended by what seems like a trivialization of the divine.
If you must pray to find a parking space in a crowded mall
and truly believe that finding one is a "miracle" provided
by God, for heaven's sake keep it to yourself.

In fact, most nonreligious folks aren't offended by
normal manifestations of faith, nor by the more over-the-
top religiosity. (Bored, irritated, disgusted, or amused, but
rarely *offended*.) What does get their unbelieving goats? It's
this: when you assume that, because they do not believe
in God, or practice a religion, or practice a religion as
often as you do, their lives are devoid of morality,
spirituality, community, or a sense of beauty and wonder.
They're right to be offended by this, because it's insulting

---

* If you're Christian, reread the Gospels: one of the reasons people were so eager to
follow Jesus around and listen to what he said is that he was a deeply *surprising*
person. You could never predict what he would say or do. There's a good lesson in
that.

and untrue. It is entirely possible to be an ethical person without believing that one's ethics are handed down from a divine source.

Nontheists can meditate, contemplate the awesome grandeur of nature, or dwell on the infinite—and they do so just as much as religious folks. Fundamentalists find the randomness of evolution terrifying; nontheists find it a source of joy and wonder and a profound invitation to humility in the face of the awesome unlikeliness of us being here at all. If you are a believer, this may be difficult to understand, but shouldn't you also know, in your gut, that simply because something is difficult to understand, it doesn't mean it isn't real?

How to be a nonbeliever around believers

- **Treat believers with respect.** While religious people shouldn't treat atheists and agnostics as if they had no hearts, atheists and agnostics shouldn't treat religious people as if they had no brains. Just because someone says they believe in God doesn't mean they believe in an old man in the sky handing out favors and punishments. Most believers are far more nuanced than that; most are aware, too, that their religious teachings can be interpreted in many valid ways.

- **Don't assume all believers are trying to convert you.** Don't leap to the conclusion that every religious person is a zealot longing to bring you into the fold. Be gracious when someone says he'll pray for you if you are sick or mourning. Seeing another person suffer without being able to do anything about it is a terrible experience; whether you believe in prayer or not, why deny someone the comfort of feeling that they can at least do something on your behalf?

- **Don't hide your own nonbeliefs.** By the same token, you need never be in the closet as a nonbeliever—in fact, you do *believe*, just not in a religion. If you feel you must, for tactical reasons, keep your atheism (or other nonreligious identity) to yourself because you would face discrimination, that's one thing, but in terms of morals and politeness, there's no reason to do so: there's nothing inherently rude or confrontational about stating that you don't believe in God or religion.

The Principles of Good Faith

Question: *A few years ago, some of my neighbors joined a New Age religious order that requires them to change their first names every so often. Some are already on their third incarnation. Because I have a hard time remembering names and don't know if I really want to endorse my neighbors' religious choice, I've been avoiding calling them anything except "Hey you." Am I being rude?*

Oh, America! When it comes to religion we are diverse, we are devout, we are tolerant, and we are pig-ignorant. Most people don't know anything at all about the beliefs, practices, or demographic numbers of non-Christians; plenty don't know much about any tradition other than their own; and a not-insignificant group don't even know what their own religion teaches. We think Sodom and Gomorrah were married, that Jesus was born in Jerusalem, that Billy Graham preached the Sermon on the Mount. We can't name more than five of the Ten Commandments. We're just out there loving God and our neighbors for all we're worth and not bothering terribly much about our homework. Frankly, it's sort of endearing, even if it can lead to the occasional faux pas.

How can you act in good faith?

- **Engage (other) religions as more than labels.** In general it's a bad idea to assume, because you know someone is an atheist, a Baptist, a Muslim, a Hindu, or whatever else, that you know anything else about them. There is so much diversity within *all* traditions that merely knowing someone's label doesn't entitle you to make assumptions about how they feel about the afterlife, the origin of their scriptures, sexual morality, gender roles, global warming, the Middle East, abortion, other religions, or the appropriateness of white shoes after Labor Day. (It's true that *most* Episcopalians have a problem with that, but every now and then you run into a renegade, and it's rude to call their faith into question.) Just about anyone gets irritated when they hear, "Oh, well, as an X, you surely must do/believe/care about Y." They'll get annoyed even if you happen to be right in their particular case, because they know so many Xs who don't, and don't like hearing their fellows stereotyped. Often, and ironically, this mistake is made in the cause of religious tolerance, trying to show the "other" that you *get* them. Don't try. Graceful ignorance is so much better than clueless attempts at understanding.

- **Treat (other) religious beliefs with respect.** So what *should* you call your New Age neighbors who change their names out of religious conviction? The most polite thing is to address people as they wish to be addressed.* However, people who change their first names, or anything else, on a regular basis (not a habit most people keep up past the teenage years, but so be it) need to be prepared to be extremely patient with the mistakes of others, regardless of the religious motivation behind it. You should feel free to ask for reminders about religious beliefs as often as you need to. For instance, perhaps the New Age order requires frequent name changes in order to cultivate tolerance and detachment in its followers, and other people's confusion plays a key role in your neighbors' spiritual development. Perhaps.

   But you also needn't fear you're tacitly approving of a religious belief by interacting with a believer on their own terms, say, by using their preferred nom du jour or letting them pass on that pork dish. Addressing people by their chosen names doesn't imply approval of the name itself or the reasons for its choice, just as respecting someone's food rules doesn't convert you to their religion. For example, if a female friend got married and changed her name, you wouldn't refuse to use her married name because you didn't like her husband, or found her old name more euphonious, or believed she is perpetuating the patriarchy. Of course, this also assumes that a religious belief is respectful of your

---

* For the record, many people in the city don't bother learning their neighbors' names at all, and some use nomenclature that might be classified as pungent. So "Hey you" is well ahead of the politeness curve to begin with.

own beliefs. If your neighbors' New-Age-order-approved names are fairly mainstream, like Timmy or Voldemort, or if they're restrained by food rules, that's one thing. If they're calling themselves things like Angelchild Messiah or Krishna Godfollower or forcing you to break your own food rules—in other words, if they are impinging on your beliefs—then that's a different story. In that case, you're best off excusing yourself from the situation or addressing them as Mr. and Ms. Zealot (or whatever). No one can quibble with the politeness of that. (If the New Age order starts changing their last names, too, you might want to embrace your inner Mr. Rogers and start addressing them as "Neighbor.")

• **Attend (other) religious ceremonies with respect.** Presumably, you treat your own religious observances with engaged respect (at least most of the time; we all have days when we're just not into it). Other people's religious observances are best treated with disengaged respect; that is, you honor their beliefs while not compromising your own. Some etiquette books say you should not wear a symbol of your own religion when attending a ceremony of a different religion. That's wrongheaded. Obviously, you don't show up at a mosque wearing a blingishly big Jesus fish or attend a Hindu wedding in a "Mary Is My Homegirl" T-shirt (not that you should be attending a wedding in a T-shirt, anyway), but subtler expressions—those that are about *you*, not about trying to proselytize to the heathens—are perfectly fine. For one thing, while a crucifix necklace is optional, not all religious symbols are; yarmulkes or head scarfs are considered mandatory by those who wear them. For another, it can be helpful to let folks know you're not a member of the team, so they'll know to help you out and understand your choice not to participate in certain rituals. During my Catholic-school-teaching years, taking communion was highly politicized. Because of this, I always wore my Star of David necklace at events where communion was served to let people know that I wasn't making a point about abortion or John Kerry or the sex-abuse scandal, I just wasn't Catholic. I appreciate seeing people with head scarfs or crucifix necklaces at my synagogue when we do interfaith events so that I can introduce myself and tell them where the restrooms are and ask if there's anything about the service they'd like explained (all while praying I'll know the answer).

• **Do some homework in advance.** If you're going to attend a service of a religion that you don't belong to, ask someone in advance what's expected—what everyone is supposed to do to show respect, and what is only to be done by members. In many synagogues, for example, all men are expected to wear yarmulkes, and if you don't have your own, a basket of hideously unattractive cheap satin ones is provided. Wear one; it doesn't make you Jewish, it just makes you a nipplehead. At Christian churches, on the other hand, only observing Christians take communion, and it's an offense to their faith and your own (or lack thereof) to do so if you're not a Christian yourself. You need never say words that you disbelieve in (participating in a call-and-response at a Christian service, for example) nor, if it makes you physically or psychologically uncomfortable, kneel. On the other hand, don't make yourself conspicuous: remain seated, close your eyes when others pray, and maintain a pleasant countenance. If you're ever asked to do something that makes you uncomfortable, like saying grace over dinner, a simple, "I'm not comfortable with that" should do you fine.

- **Indulge your curiosity.** It is also okay to ask religious folk (or nonreligious folk, for that matter) questions about their beliefs and practices. There is one true belief that underlies all religions and philosophical systems, and it is this: *we are sorely misunderstood.* Give people a chance to rectify that sense of misunderstanding, and they will love you forever. Obviously, you ask when the situation is right—in an appropriate setting, not at the annual staff meeting, and when the feelings of peace and camaraderie are regnant, not immediately after an acrimonious debate about Intelligent Design.

  And ask in the right way. Make it clear from your tone and wording that you are not trying to trap them into saying something stupid or self-contradictory, nor are you looking to make fun of them. Make it clear, also, that you're not interested in converting. "I've always been interested in religious diversity. Could I ask you about . . ." is a nice way to start, except that it sounds like a horribly prepackaged etiquette-guide script of how people *should* talk rather than the way they actually do. The idea is to let the person know that your interest is genuine and respectful, and not about your personal spiritual needs. Find your own natural words for opening the conversation.

- **Respond calmly and kindly to proselytizers.** Of course, sometimes there's no need to ask, because a religious person won't shut up about his beliefs long enough for you to get a word in edgewise. If he's talking primarily about himself—how much Jesus has done for *him*, the glories of *his* latest meditation retreat—then treat him like any monomaniacal talker: give a lot of "uh-huh" and "how nice" responses. (For detailed advice on how not to get hijacked by monomaniacs, see chapter 7.)

Assume that someone who talks about religion a lot, or prays for you, isn't trying to convert you. If people want to pray for you in times of trouble, let them, even if you are a nonbeliever or don't believe in their religion. It's a way for them to harness their emotional energy on your behalf and to not feel practically helpless in the face of suffering. Stifling this natural urge is cruel and pointless—and promotes negative stereotypes about nonbelievers. It's ungracious to reject a person's natural enthusiasms or soulful support.

If, however, he *is* trying to convert you, it will drive him absolutely batty if you're not noticing, so it's a win-win. If someone is trying to convert you in a more overt way—by inviting you to Bible study or a meditation retreat, or casually mentioning that he is praying for the salvation of your soul—politely ask him to stop. Don't argue; this will only invite more convoluted arguments for why you should convert. (Nobody decides to go off on a mission without doing some prep work. Whatever your initial objections might be, he's heard them, and he's got answers. You may not think they're *good* answers, but they're answers.) Whatever you do, don't get angry; your inability to control your emotions will only further convince him that you are an unenlightened soul who must be saved.

To calmly disengage from evangelical entreaties, try something along the lines of, "I realize this is important to you and you have the best wishes for me. I have my philosophical/religious beliefs and they're not going to change because of what you say. Please be assured that I've heard your message, you've done your best." If you're being proselytized by a Christian, you might add, "You can shake the dust off your feet." He'll get it. If he doesn't, kindheartedly suggest, "Matthew 10:14."* The Gospels do say that Christians are supposed to spread the word but also make it clear that they're not supposed to keep spreading it over and over in the same place like a toddler with jam, so use that to your advantage. Whatever the religion of the proselytizer, your best approach involves "You've done all you can; if there is to be change in me it's in God's hands now" rather than an aggressive "Back off!"

If a person continues to proselytize after you've had the talk, warn once and then take action. If you're dealing with a coworker, tell him—with the preface that you know he is acting out of goodwill toward you—that you will consider any future attempts to be harassment and will document and report it to management accordingly. If you're dealing with a friend, let him know that continued attempts to change your belief system will make it difficult to continue your relationship. If the friend continues to try, break up: "I can't be friends with someone who won't respect my beliefs."

If you're dealing with a family member—well, that's a

---

* The New International Version Bible translates this verse as: "If anyone will not welcome you or listen to your words, shake the dust off your feet when you leave that home or town."

lot tougher, isn't it? I can't give a simple recommendation for that because every situation is so different, and "breaking up," as difficult as it is with a friend, may not even be possible with a relative. A highly customized version of the above, though, should help guide you through your particular situation. If the nagger is of a fundamentalist stripe, do your best to have compassion while asserting your boundaries. After all, if he believes salvation is only achievable through his particular brand of God, then he genuinely believes that you are at risk of being *tortured forever*. Tortured. Forever. Just think about that for a minute. Can you imagine thinking that might happen to someone you love and standing by as though it didn't matter? I can't imagine anything more horrible. So be gentle, and remember that whatever annoyances a proselytizer is inflicting on you surely pale in comparison to the pain he hopes to save you from—and is putting himself through, at that.

The Christmas Conundrum

"I do like Christmas on the whole. . . . In its clumsy way, it does approach Peace and Goodwill. But it is clumsier every year."

—E. M. Forster, *Howards End*

Every December, the letters start pouring in. To Santa, and to Miss Conduct.

Christmas is particularly confusing to navigate because no one can really agree on just how religious a holiday it is. Just as Jews are both a religious group and an ethnic group—thereby confusing everybody including, at times, ourselves—Christmas is both a religious holiday and a secular one: Jesus Christmas and Santa Christmas.

Plenty of non-Christians celebrate Santa Christmas, feeling that it's a big, commercial, fun holiday and no more against their own beliefs than a birthday party would be. Some Christians don't celebrate Christmas at all, believing that since the Bible doesn't say Jesus was born on December 25 (he was probably born in the spring), celebrating his birth on that day is wrong. Other Christians agree but figure that Santa Christmas is still, as it were, kosher, or that even if Jesus wasn't born on Christmas Day, there's nothing wrong with letting a couple thousand years of tradition set the date on which to celebrate his birth.

Which is all to say that it's ridiculously reductionist—and just plain not true—when the megaphoned "War on Christmas" crowd starts pounding its annual drums like a corps of enraged, demented little drummer boys. There is no war on Christmas. See the lights? Hear the music, starting sometime in early November? Note the time off work—or the overtime, if you're unfortunate enough to work in retail? Fall prey to the commercials? Christmas isn't going anywhere. In fact, I'm tempted to think that perhaps there *should* be a war on Christmas, given the war that Christmas wages on Americans' wallets, blood-sugar levels, personal serenity, family peace, and ability to manage addictions. But then, asking an advice columnist her opinion of Christmas is kind of like asking an ER nurse her opinion of motorcycles. We never see the stories with a happy ending.

Whether you're a believer in Santa Christmas, Jesus Christmas, both, or neither, be smarter than to buy into the "War on Christmas" hype. As a religious holiday, Christmas celebrates the miracle of God entering the world as an infant born in a stable, naked, poor, and powerless. The most beloved secular myths of

Christmas also advocate treating the poor (Bob Cratchit), the different (Rudolph), and the humble (Charlie Brown's Christmas tree) with respect and compassion. Either way, wishing a "Merry, Militant Christmas" to everyone you meet stands against the spirit of the day. Instead, show Christmas spirit to those who don't celebrate—or who don't celebrate as you do. Particularly, don't get snooty with salesclerks who wish you "Happy Holidays." You're not standing up for some grand principle by responding "Merry Christmas!" in a snarky tone; you're just being impolite to someone making minimum wage at a harried time of the year.

When it comes to your social equals—those who aren't obliged to smile at you—wishing people joy on a holiday they don't celebrate is somewhat pointless. It's like the way little kids sometimes get confused on the birthday concept and wish *you* a happy birthday on *their* birthdays. Or like the spam e-mails I constantly receive, promising me a larger male organ. Look, you can wish me a Merry Christmas or a larger penis all you want: I'll never, ever have one. And I'm okay with that.

But I'm not militant about it, either, because as a non-Christmas person I know I'm in an extreme minority. I also know that being wished "Merry Christmas" is hardly the same thing as being baptized and forced to recite the catechism at gunpoint. If you are a Muslim, Wiccan, Buddhist, or random heathen who is wished "Merry Christmas," either blow it off with a casual, "You, too!" or look at it as an opportunity to espouse your values by telling your well-wisher how you plan to spend December 25:

- "Thanks! I'll be subbing for one of my colleagues at the hospital so she can be with her family."

- "Merry Christmas to you, too. My friends and I always get together for Chinese food and a movie."
- "I can't wait. Christmas is one of the few days of the year I have time to get to the mosque for all five prayers!"

There's obviously nothing wrong with wishing someone a Merry Christmas if that's what they celebrate. If the O'Malleys invite the Cohens over for their annual Christmas party, there's no reason for a stilted round of "Happy Holidays" at the end of it. The Cohens can wish the O'Malleys a Merry Christmas and the O'Malleys can wish the Cohens a Happy Hanukkah. And the O'Malleys aren't fooling the Cohens or making them feel more included by labeling their Christmas party a "holiday" party. If the decorations are red and green and there's a "secret pal" gift exchange, it's not a "holiday" party, it's a Christmas party, and you may as well call it such. Claiming that the red and green lights in the office are "holiday" decorations is also disingenuous. There is no other holiday in December that features red and green lights but Christmas (Traffic Light Day?).

Non-Christians aren't particularly concerned that neither Santa nor the Easter Bunny is in the Bible. Santa and the Easter Bunny are symbols of holidays attached to a religion that they don't practice. Some people are comfortable separating the secular and religious aspects of such holidays, others aren't. It's okay to say "I'm sorry, I'm not comfortable with Christmas parties," and not attend them—just as it would be okay for a conservative Christian to decide that she's not comfortable with Halloween, as many aren't, and choose not to go to a party for that. Support folks who are up front about their discomfort with holidays that aren't part of their religious or ethnic heritage, and who politely decline an invitation. They're being grown-up about it. What, you'd rather they show up and be a complete buzz kill?

Even among people who do celebrate the same holidays, conflicts can arise when they celebrate them in different ways. The holidays that stick around do so because they're open to so many different interpretations and celebratory practices: Jesus Christmas and Santa Christmas, Jesus Easter and Bunny Easter. Thanksgiving can be gemütlich or gourmet. Halloween can be as child- or adult-centered as your lifestyle dictates. Independence Day can be about patriotism or picnics. So don't insist on a "right" interpretation, and when you are going to celebrate the holidays with friends or new family for the first time, communicate in advance about expectations. Ironically, interfaith couples often have it easier with this one, because they realize that they will need to discuss and negotiate. People from similar backgrounds can take their traditions for granted, leading to unpleasant surprises when Edward expects everyone gathered around the Thanksgiving table to say grace and share what they're grateful for that year, and Josie expects them to keep their mouths shut and watch the game.

Be willing to adapt to others whom you love, and be willing to adapt to your own needs over time, as well. Just as ways of celebrating the holidays differ from person to person, they differ year by year. If you haven't celebrated Hanukkah since childhood, but this year you are in special need of spiritual rededication, break out the menorah and prayer books. Or if you have suffered a loss in your family and just can't bring yourself to do the traditional Thanksgiving at Aunt Bessie's, why not suggest the family go to a restaurant instead? Just as you shouldn't make others feel guilty or inadequate for not celebrating the holidays the way you do, you shouldn't make yourself feel bad for not celebrating them the way you have in the past.

Holiday traditions are lovely, but they shouldn't be a straitjacket. Instead, they should be more like a really great pair of black trousers—something that goes with everything and with which you can be creative. Don't forget, there's nothing wrong with including *yourself* among those for whom you are extending tolerance.

· 4 ·

She Said, He Said

SEX AND RELATIONSHIPS

"'Fair, kind, and true' have often liv'd alone
Which three till now, never kept seat in one."
—William Shakespeare, Sonnet 105

Finding love has never been easy. Apparently the old college dating rule, "Smart, sane, or sexy: pick two," has been around since Shakespeare's time. And popular advice about love is as likely to make the situation more difficult as it is to smooth the path to true romance.

There are few areas in which we invest as many of our fears and hopes as we do in sex, relationships, and our sexual and gender identity—and few areas of modern life that have changed as much in the past fifty years. You can no longer assume that:

- Men are to desire.
- Women are to be desired.
- Men do the asking, paying, and proposing.
- Women flirt and follow the rules.

- Women deserve and require protection.
- Men deserve and require deference.
- Sexual attraction is the basis for any nonfamilial relationships between men and women.
- Everyone is straight.
- People are virgins until they get married.
- The third date is the inevitable "booty date."
- Romance requires flowers, candlelight, expensive dinners, and jewelry.
- Everyone wants to get married.
- Everyone has One True Love.
- Any relationships before the One True Love arrives are regrettable mistakes.
- Getting married is the entryway to adulthood.
- Marriage leads to children.
- Old people are "past" sex.

In actual fact, you never really *could* assume any of these things; there was just a societal consensus of "how things were," and even if the official version didn't match up with their own experience, people went along with it. We MacGyvered our public sex lives as best we could, pulling together bits of accepted dating etiquette and wedding protocol that may have had little connection to our personal desires. When Freud spoke of "work and love" as the requirements for human happiness, he nailed it: Nearly everyone wants to be respected in the public sphere, and almost all of us want a chance at a life with someone who will love, honor, and cherish us.

Nobody ever guaranteed those things would come together easily.

The goal of this chapter is to deal with some of the major ways that changing and diverse notions of gender can trip us up on that quest for work and love. I will not be dealing with intimate relationships, because Miss Conduct isn't a relationship columnist or a sex columnist; I'm an etiquette columnist. The point of etiquette isn't to get along with your significant other, it's to get along with *everyone*. So I'll deal with romance right up to your first date, and then draw a discreet curtain and leave you to proceed more intimately. We will, however, discuss how to handle the publicly visible—and audible—romances of others, and how to avoid engendering misconceptions, miscommunications, and missteps in your nonromantic life.

(I'm also not a lawyer. So, just as I didn't include poisoning in the food chapter, I won't be covering major issues such as acquaintance rape, sexual harassment, gay bashing, or sexual discrimination. Those who need advice in these areas should seek legal resources.)

Finally, a word about terminology: Except when I'm talking specifically about gay folks, I'm going to use language that applies to heterosexuals, for which I apologize. It doesn't reflect any disdain for gay people but rather my sense, based on the letters I receive, that straight folks, however easier our lives are in many ways, have choppier waters to navigate romantically. It's no easier to find love if you're gay, but at least you don't have to deal with the incomprehensibility of the opposite sex, or the obtuseness of self-help books attempting to help you comprehend same, in quite the same way beleaguered straight folks do. Some of my advice (such as the courtesies singles and couples owe each other) applies to people of all sexual orientations; some doesn't. You'll know when what I'm talking about applies to your situation and when it doesn't.

To Hold the Door or Not to Hold the Door

One of the most vexing contemporary questions of etiquette is, Should one practice gender-based or gender-neutral etiquette?

We all embrace equality in some areas and traditionalism in others. There are patriarchal dads who proudly cheer their daughters' accomplishments on the soccer field, stay-at-home moms who volunteer as escorts at abortion clinics, hard-charging career women who love to sink into regressive bodice rippers at the end of long days prosecuting deadbeat dads, men who vociferously supported Hillary Clinton but still feel uncomfortable letting a woman pay on a date. It depends on who we're with and what we're doing. It's not as though there are "perfect feminists" in one camp and "perfect traditionalists" in another.

Generally, though, society is adopting gender-neutral manners, with respect and consideration expressed in the same way to men and women alike, at least in work and neutral public settings. But there are still those who practice gendered etiquette, whether out of personal belief or simple habit. And one person's chivalry is another person's condescension, one person's common sense is another's disrespect.

If you prefer gendered etiquette, know that occasionally women will appear to be unappreciative (if you are male) and men will appear to be uncaring (if you are female). I wouldn't recommend a romantic relationship with someone who has a gender ideology much different from your own, but with friends, neighbors, and coworkers, it's best to judge behavior in context: is Dave in tech support just rude when he doesn't open the door for you when you think he should (or does open it when you think he shouldn't) or is he typically a bit thoughtless and fond of microwaving broccoli for lunch?

If you're a man who follows gendered etiquette:

- make a special effort to show that your chivalry is based on respect for women (or, as is sometimes the case, your self-image as a gallant type) and not on contempt;
- listen when women talk;
- treat women as experts when they are experts; and
- be scrupulously fair in your dealings.

If you're a woman who follows gendered etiquette:

- make a special effort to show that your traditionalism isn't just a cover story for freeloading;
- take on leadership roles when you're the logical choice to do so; and
- be securely competent (not some latter-day Blanche DuBois) in your dealings.

If you follow gender-neutral etiquette, be patient with those who don't—especially older people. Yes, Ms. Marathoner ought to give up her subway seat to that eighty-year-old man, but he might not be able to bring himself to accept it. It's more about him than her, so she should go ahead and sit back down. Stand up for yourself when you are the target of actual condescension or advantage-taking, not when you are confronted by the symbols of it. There are plenty of perfectly nice men who insist on opening doors and women who prefer to be paid for on dates, and plenty of rotters who treat everyone with utterly equal and aboveboard disdain. Don't mistake symbol for substance.

What to Call People

"I have a name. It's Dorothy. It's not Tootsie or Toots or Sweetie or Honey or Doll. . . . Alan's always Alan, Tom's always Tom, and John's always John. I have a name, too."
—*Tootsie*

A rose by any other name may smell as sweet, but a Rosemary addressed as Rosie might feel decidedly thorny. Misses, ma'ams and Mses, guys and gals, and dudes—how to appropriately address individuals and groups of all ages is a tricky matter.

One on one
First and foremost, call people by their *names*:

- **Avoid nicknames and endearments.** Nicknames aren't appropriate unless you know someone awfully well. Don't use them in the workplace, ever (unless nicknaming is part of the overall work culture and everyone—and I mean *everyone*, except, perhaps, the boss—gets one). Endearments are out of bounds. No "hons," "sweeties," or "babes," unless you're a tough-talking but tenderhearted diner waitress. Feel free to object to any nickname you don't much like, optimally by replying to "Hey, sweetie?" with "Yes, pookie?"

- **Only use diminutives if that's the person's preference.** Refer to a person, especially a woman, by whatever version of her name she uses—no arrogating to yourself the right to dub Elizabeth "Liz" or Margaret "Peggy." Most women tend to have strong aesthetic preferences about their names, and you're on treacherous ground if you call a grown-up Susan "Sue," or worse "Suzy," and she associates that name with childhood (and being treated *as a child*). If you are a Susan—or a Jonathan or Timothy, for that matter—who gets undesirably truncated, keep correcting people, cheerfully and relentlessly, until they get it right. Everyone knows a dozen Sues, Daves, and Beths, so it can take a while to learn a new acquaintance's preference.

- **Pick the best formal address.** In the old days, marital context determined formal address: unmarried women were Miss Mary Sunshine, married women were Mrs. John Raindrops, and divorced women were Mrs. Sunshine Raindrops. Today's woman has these and as many other options as you can imagine to choose from, which can make addressing an envelope to her rather difficult. In workplace situations, it's best to go with "Ms. Mary Sunshine" (assuming Mary isn't a doctor, judge, or rabbi) because Mary's marital status isn't relevant to her business identity. For social correspondence, rely on your knowledge of Mary—for example, it's a good chance that if she and her husband have different last names, she's a Ms. If they have the same names and you don't really know how Mary feels about such things, go with whatever your own preferences are. If Mary and John divorce, ask her what name she's going by, and if she goes back to Sunshine, never mention Raindrops again. Mary, for her part, ought not to get in a snit about envelopes addressed in a way that don't conform exactly to her notions of gentility and equality. She ought to be glad, in this day of e-mail and text messaging, that anyone is bothering to write to her at all.

- **Respect that it's *her* last name.** A woman who decides to keep her own name when she gets married should have her decision respected, and in this case "respected" means not questioned or commented upon at all. It doesn't matter how you feel about women changing or keeping their names; what matters is how the couple themselves feel about it. You can assume that whatever the woman's decision, they feel just fine, and that if they don't it's none of your business. If you are interrogated about your own surname status, respond in a way that indicates the sheer presumption of the question: "It's a good thing I didn't need your permission, then," or "We're all comfortable with our names, thanks," ought to do it. Ideally you'll sound as though you're not quite sure they're really asking what they seem to be asking, but you have decided to humor them anyway. Similarly, if you are a diehard feminist and a friend changes her name, back off. You don't know what the change symbolizes to her—maybe it's a way of saying good-bye to her past, or a purely aesthetic decision.

The group

The polite term of address for women whose name you don't know and which terms can be properly used to address a group of women are matters of bitter controversy.* Every time I answer a question in my column about the use of "miss"

---

* Collective nouns are less problematic. No group of women wants to be referred to as a "gaggle." "Bevy," however, can be oddly flattering.

or "ma'am," or whether one can address one's female friends as "you guys," I get letters. *Tons* of letters, taking all possible positions and all vociferously declaiming that this particular position is the only possible correct one.

Which means one thing, for sure: *Do not ever blame or undertip waitstaff for calling you something you don't like. Ever.* You're just a horrible person if you do that. The twenty-first-century dilemmas of prescriptive linguistics and changing gender norms are not the fault of people whose job it is to bring you food and refill your water glass. So whether you're greeted as "miss" or "ma'am" or "you guys"—ignore it, and get on with your life. Or correct the server, nicely but firmly, and then leave a good tip so that he or she knows you weren't mad.

- **Address women as adults.** Although I generally don't make a lot of headway on this, I'd like to urge non-Southern women to rethink their widespread prejudice about being called "ma'am."* It isn't an acronym for "Menopausal, Aging, and Moody," it's an appropriate term of address for any adult woman. "Ma'am" makes no presumption about a woman's marital status, nor about her age, except that she is a grown-up. "Ma'am" is the feminine equivalent of "Sir," which is why women in the military are addressed as "Ma'am." How silly would it be to call a full colonel "Miss"?

  In contrast, "girls" is a term best used exclusively among women. It's slightly over-chummy, but not insulting, for a waitress to say, "You girls ready to order?" It is insulting for a waiter to do so, especially if he is a decade or more

---

* And to congratulate Southern women on their thoroughly sensible attitudes.

younger than the "girls" in question. (Though, again, you *don't not tip* because of this; maybe the last table he waited on was absolutely delighted to be called "girls.") There are certain words, and certain jokes, that only people inside the group get to use or make.

- **Be chill with guys and dudes.** The appropriateness of addressing women as "guys" is something of a hot button. I'm generally not bothered by it, perhaps because I'm a Midwesterner. You wouldn't address or refer to an individual woman as a "guy," of course, but across large stretches of the United States, "guy" is masculine in the singular and neuter in the plural.

  While "guys" can only be used to address a group of women, "dude" can be used to address an individual woman. This is because "dude" serves not only as a term of address but one of intensification, dismay, delight, and any other emotion you can think of. "Dude, I got the job!" when addressed to a man is the equivalent of "Dave, I got the job!"; addressed to a woman, it's more like "Hooray! I got the job." There's no need to get peevish about it. People who say "dude" at all tend to say "dude" a lot, and they might also tend to have somewhat impaired memories (for various reasons) and will find it difficult to recall that you alone of all their friends are not a dude. So you'd best learn to live with it.

- **Remember that people are nouns.** Don't refer to men and women as "males" or "females" unless you want to save the opposite sex some time by broadcasting right from the get-go how much you hate them. "Male" and "female" are adjectives; as nouns, they are only appropriate for animals. Referring to people thusly makes it sound as though you regard them as livestock or lab rats. And for the love of all that's holy, don't ever refer to people of a race not your own as "black males" or "white females" unless you want the world to know how racist *and* sexist you are.

The plus one

It's a sad fact that there are no dignified words for romantic partners to whom one is not married. "Boyfriend" and "girlfriend" are all right until you're twenty-five or so but problematic after that. "Lover" is fine if you're Simone de Beauvoir talking about Jean-Paul Sartre but unbearably pretentious for anyone else. "Partner" is rather clinical (although it's taken on sufficient popularity that when you're talking about your business partner, these days, you'd better say "business partner"), and anyway doesn't work for relationships that haven't reached an official stage; you're not someone's "partner" after the third date. On the other side of the spectrum, "plus one" has a terrifically temporary feeling to it, as though the relationship will expire at the end of the evening, like Cinderella's pumpkin coach. "Significant other" works nicely but has an oddly theoretical cast to it; you hear people talking about significant others in the abstract, but never about their own particular one. "Sweetie" appears to be gaining popularity and has the advantages of being gender-neutral, affectionate, casual, and silly enough to communicate, "There's no good words for who this person is to me." I rather like "consort," myself, but you have to display a certain panache to pull that off. The best solution is to introduce or refer to your significant other as soon as possible, so that afterward you can simply refer to him or her by name.

Gay people use the same words to refer to their significant others as straight people do. A married woman is a wife, regardless of the sex of the person she's married to, and a married man is a husband. Of course, any married people can be "spouses" if they like.

Pronoun politesse

People who have had gender reassignment surgery or are in the process of changing sex are referred to as the gender they are switching to, even if you are describing something they did before the change. Transsexuals don't see themselves as people who have gotten a sex *change*, they see themselves as people who have, later in life than they might have wished, been able to match their outward selves to their inward ones. So a male-to-female transsexual, for example, is referred to as "she" in the present day, and also when referring to her presurgery days.

Always use gender-neutral language in the workplace and ideally everywhere else, too. Theoretically, yes, "he" and "man" and "mankind" when used in the abstract refer to women as well, but cognitively they don't. Experiment after experiment has shown that when people read a sentence such as "If a student wants to succeed, he should develop good study habits" or "All men are created equal," they think about *men*, not *people*. This kind of language in the workplace sends the not-too-subtle signal that women aren't really considered part of the team. So use "he or she," switch between "he" and "she," or just rewrite the sentence: "Students who want to succeed need good study habits"—which nicely reinforces the universality of the sentiment and doesn't posit striving for academic achievement as one lonely man's eccentricity.

Romances: Your Own

"Who is it that says most, which can say more
Than this rich praise, that you alone are you."
—William Shakespeare, Sonnet 84

You want to find that special someone, right, and not that special anyone? That someone who alone is he or she? Then you might want to stay away from magazine articles that promise to tell you the secrets of the opposite sex. Being highly skeptical of universal claims about male and female nature is one of those rare practices that is both good manners and good science. Gender differences are real, but individual differences are realer, and you're not dating "men" or "women," you're dating one man or one woman.*

Learn to listen and pay attention to the actual person you're with and keep away from books promising to translate the opposite sex for you. Anthropological field guides make sense if you're trying to comprehend the rituals of the remote tribes of the Andaman Islands, but why on earth would you need them to figure out what makes 50 percent of your own culture tick? These kinds of books can become a too-easy shortcut that makes you feel you "get" men or women without bothering to get to know them, which is both insulting and almost certain to come back and bite you. Even if a book is right in a particular case, no one wants to feel as though they're being managed like a clinical specimen of "Man" or "Woman"; they want to feel appreciated and cared for as Jack or Diane.

---

* Or more than one. It's none of my business how many people you date—as long as they all know about one another. The point is that you're not dating a statistical composite.

So listen to people and believe them. If a woman says she doesn't like flowers, don't bring her flowers. If a man says he hates sports, don't surprise him with tickets to the hockey play-offs.

Making the first move

It's hard to try to appeal to the opposite sex. The people that you're interested in aren't always interested in you—which is true of gay folks, too, of course, and has been the sorry state of love since the beginning of time. What's new over the past few decades is that advertising and media have taken an unprecedented role in explaining exactly what is wrong with you if you can't find a mate: you're not thin enough, not muscular enough, not rich enough, not adventurous enough, not feminine enough, not masculine enough. So in addition to being lonely, you hate yourself. And then it becomes all too easy to start hating the opposite sex for their unrealistic expectations.

That's a place to which you don't want to go. Being single and straight and not wanting to be the former is a normal state of affairs. When you're single and straight and not wanting to be the latter, that's when you need to pull your head out of pop culture for a while. The actual men and women of the opposite sex aren't your problem. The problem is the media, which have at the time of this writing determined that the only couple in the world who deserve to mate are Brad Pitt and Angelina Jolie. The rest of us deserve only to read about them and spend our money on products that promise to bring us an eyebrow hair closer to their unearthly beauty.

So put down the magazines, turn off the television, and go for a walk. Take a look at the couples you see. Are they all fab-ulously attractive? Are they all terribly wealthy? Do none of them ever get hair in places considered inappropriate to their sex or fail to have hair in places considered mandatory? There are a handful of neighborhoods in Los Angeles where the answer to all three of these questions, on any given day outside hiatus season, is likely "yes." If you live in one of these areas, take frequent field trips; it'll be good for your mental health. In general, however, the answer is no. Stay in touch with that reality, as much as you can. Don't give up on yourself, or love, or the opposite sex. Just give up on magazines that promise to teach you ten tips to leave him, or her, begging for more. Instead, try these three tips for surviving the dating scene:

- **Don't underestimate the opposite sex.** Both sexes tend to hold exaggerated and stereotypical notions of the other's preferences. Women overestimate men's preference for thinness, muscle definition, large breasts, and full lips—which might explain why more than two million tubes of lipstick are purchased *each day* in the United States, according to Harvard psychologist Nancy Etcoff.

  Men, on the other hand, overestimate how important big muscles—and a big penis—are to women. One study compared the muscle mass of men's bodies depicted in *Cosmopolitan* and in *Men's Health* magazines to women's and men's ideals, that is, what women identified as the ideal muscle mass in a sex partner versus what men believed was a woman's ideal man.* The ranking, from least muscular to most muscular:

---

* The study included this classic line: "We made color photocopies of the front covers of *Men's Health, Men's Fitness,* and *Muscle & Fitness,* and the monthly 'Hunk of the Month with His Shirt Off' centerfold in *Cosmpolitan*." Ah, life in the ivory tower. You just know the professors were embarrassed to go buy those magazines themselves and made some poor grad student do it.

1. *Cosmopolitan*
2. women's ideal
3. men's expectation of women's ideal
4. *Men's Health*

And if a man is worried about his hairline, two words: Patrick Stewart. Short, bald, and *still* considered by many women the sexiest man alive even though he's almost seventy. Is there any woman who would prefer the conventionally macho First Officer William T. Riker to Captain Jean-Luc Picard?*

• **Do your best with what you've got.** Don't get too worked up when the evolutionary psychology crowd preaches the gospel of beauty conquering all. Looks matter in a lot of situations and there's no getting around it. But do you know the major theory du jour in evolutionary circles about the purpose of beauty? Parasites. As in showing that you don't have any. Apparently, a major reason that facial symmetry, clear skin, lustrous hair, and all the rest are attractive is because they show that you're not suffering from tapeworms, lice, and their ilk. You aren't, are you? Well, there you go: evolutionarily speaking, you're gorgeous. The next time you feel down about your receding hairline or descending rear end, look at yourself in the mirror and affirm in a loud, clear, confident voice: "I do not look like a person riddled with pathogenic parasites." That ought to get your self-esteem up in time for the speed-dating event.

---

* Most men I know strongly preferred the butch-cut, aggressive Tasha Yar to the submissive, stereotypical bombshell Deanna Troi, too. Also note Ginger versus Mary Ann; Jennifer versus Bailey.

You want your self-esteem up, too, because that's going to be your major selling point. Beauty of face and figure, the kind that can be captured in photographs, is known as "static" beauty. Because it's easy to record and quantify, that's what psychologists have mostly studied. But there is also dynamic beauty—expressive skills, confidence, posture, movement—and these elements, we're finding, are just as crucial to attraction.

So no fair spending all your time playing Second Life or watching *The Bachelor*, rambling around in your comfort sweats, and then complaining that no one appreciates the real you. Apparently you don't either, because you're not treating yourself with much love. A good job helps— not one where you make fabulous amounts of money, necessarily, but one that gives you joy and something to talk about with other people. Some interesting life stories and hobbies. Good grooming and a sense of personal style. Some useful skills you can show off when appropriate, from emergency first aid to vegetarian cooking to PhotoShop wizardry. (Showing off your PhotoShop wizardry by taking fifteen pounds off your Match.com profile picture is not an appropriate use of your skill.) Confidence, empathy, and a genuine affection for the opposite sex. Plus at least a couple of excellent features—shiny, well-cut hair, good skin, a room-lighting smile, a toned physique, lively eye contact make people realize what that "mirror of the soul" thing is all about. You *can* have all that stuff. Maybe not the lustrous hair, if you weren't born with that, or the toned physique, if you weren't born with the capacity to acquire it. (Working out will make you look like the best you that you can be, but it won't reshape your body's fundamental parameters.) The rest of the inventory, though, just takes practice. And they're the kind of qualities that will make you attractive to *everyone*, not just potential romantic partners.

- **Don't waste too much energy in strategizing.** Some of the most entertaining research on interpersonal attraction—mostly conducted in speed-dating situations, which really are a wonderful laboratory—shows that not only do men and women not know what the opposite sex wants, they're not too clear on their own desires, either. We say we're attracted to certain qualities and then run off and snog like mad with someone who's the exact opposite. (You watched all your friends do this throughout college, and now you have science to back you up.) That article in *Maxim*—or *Psychological Science*, for that matter—telling you what men or women really want is based on self-reported anecdotes and data, and is most likely completely off the mark. Just get out there and put your best dynamic foot forward, and sooner or later a partner who wants to tango—whether he or she knew it or not—will come along.

Asking someone out

This is the single best asking-out line I have ever heard:

"I'd love to take you out for a beer sometime."

This line was addressed to my friend Ms. Coolfriend by my friend Mr. Mensch, and although Ms. Coolfriend didn't take him up on his offer, she and I both agreed that it was a remarkably good attempt. (N.B. You can do absolutely everything right and still just not be someone's type. Don't let that discourage you. Check with a few friends of the gender to which you are attracted and see if your approach is a good one. If it is, you just need to wait until the happy day when chemistry goes both ways.)

Let's break down the ingredients in Mr. Mensch's formula:

1. **"I'd love . . ."**
   The first thing you notice is that Mr. Mensch didn't actually ask Ms. Coolfriend on a date; he merely expressed his desire to do so. He made a declarative statement, not an interrogatory one. This meant that Ms. Coolfriend didn't have to flat-out reject him. She could, and did, say something like, "Oh, how nice. Well, I'll see you at the next church picnic—I've got to run now." Which allowed both of them to save face and made the next church picnic a much more comfortable affair for all concerned.

2. **"to take you out . . ."**
   This language made it perfectly clear to Ms. Coolfriend that Mr. Mensch did indeed have a romantic interest in her, that he wanted to go on a date, and intended to pay. More ambiguous statements like, "I'm going to the Winslow Homer exhibit. Would you like to come?" don't make it clear whether Mr. Mensch's primary interest is in Ms. Coolfriend or in moody New England landscapes. (Sometimes you want the ambiguity; more on this later.) Ms. Coolfriend could then choose to pursue the offer or not, in full awareness of what she was getting herself into.

3. **"for a beer . . ."**

And she wouldn't be getting herself into much. Mr. Mensch chose an activity—beer drinking—that is unpretentious, social, and requires no special skills. Nothing intimidating about getting a beer, is there? (If there is, because you're in recovery or think the object of your desire might be, then make it coffee or ice cream, obviously.) And someone who's taking you out for a beer clearly wants to get to know you. If he wanted to impress you by how much a Master of the Universe he was, he'd take you out for dinner at Chez Fancypants or scuba diving or some such. The low-key nature of the offer should make Ms. Coolfriend more likely to agree, if she's on the fence. A woman might feel awkward letting a man pay for an expensive dinner or scuba-rental equipment on what is really an "audition date," but Mr. Mensch could obviously afford a beer and maybe even some potato skins.

4. **"sometime."**

At this point the ball is lobbed squarely into Ms. Coolfriend's court. She can take Mr. Mensch up on his offer or not. Even better, she can think about it. Attraction isn't always immediate. While it had occurred to Mr. Mensch that Ms. Coolfriend was a fine figure of womanhood, perhaps she'd been distracted by her own concerns and oblivious to his charms. His clever phrasing meant that she didn't immediately have to figure out if tender feelings toward Mr. Mensch could be stirred in her ample bosom. She could make vague hand-waving motions and then call him up a few days later, if she wanted, and say, "About that beer you mentioned . . ." And if not, Mr. Mensch's casual, offhanded demeanor reassured her that she hadn't broken his heart, nor was he going to get all stalkerific on her. Ms. Coolfriend also learned that Mr. Mensch was on the market and was a smooth yet ethical operator, at that. Which might persuade Ms. Coolfriend to bring her sister or her attractive downstairs neighbor to the next church picnic, for purposes other than soul saving. Well played, Mr. Mensch.

Gentlemen, the ultimate key to succeeding in asking someone out is to make it clear that you can handle being turned down. Some men get this but take it to mean that they should come off as cool and detached or play hard to get. But it isn't that women are driven mad by the unattainable, it's that nearly every woman alive has had an unpleasant encounter with a man who expressed romantic interest and then turned nasty when she didn't respond as he wanted. Maybe it was a construction worker who followed his "Hey, baby" with a string of obscenities when she walked by without flashing a smile of gratitude. Maybe it was a professional at a conference who was full of friendly interest until he found out she had a boyfriend, at which point he suddenly wanted to network with someone else. (Because in straight courtship men still generally do the asking out, and the dynamics are different if a woman does the asking, I've stuck to the usual gender-based stereotypes.)

Regardless of the specifics, nearly every woman has had some version of this experience, and we hate it. So don't be that guy. Be the other man, the one who's cool and low-pressure and treats women like people, so that even if she's not interested she'll think, "You know, he's not for me but my friend Andrea would be all *over* this dude."

Of course, perhaps you *can't* take the object of your desire out for a beer, because she's already having one and you've just noticed her across the crowded tavern. In which case, you go and say hello. Most bars have televisions in them these days, which is a trend I hate, but the upside is that it gives you a topic of conversation: "Do you follow baseball?" "Did you happen to catch the weather report just now?" "Charlie Sheen looks exactly like my high school gym teacher and I'm starting to have PTSD dodgeball flashbacks. Would you mind nudging me when *Two and a Half Men* is over?"

This last is about as clever as you need to get. Why bother trying to figure out the perfect pick-up line? Just say something straightforward and friendly. If a woman's attracted to you, she's attracted, and if she's not, she's not. A good line can get you some *attention*, but it's not really going to sway the *evaluation*—except negatively, if you're being cocky or aggressive or manipulative. And the best lines are somewhat self-deprecating (which is why the Charlie Sheen one might just work), according to some recent research by evolutionary psychologist Gil Greengross, whose name must have provided him all kinds of opportunities for self-deprecating humor when he was in junior high.

According to Greengross, self-deprecation works because it makes the other person think about how much you're *not* like what you just said. A man making the Charlie Sheen joke is advertising his confidence, not his dodgeball deficiencies. He's also—a point gloriously missed by Greengross—advertising his harmlessness. He's saying, in effect, "I can make fun of myself for not being macho. I'm comfortable allowing you to imagine me cowering in the corner of my high school gym as balls rain down upon my head." And this is attractive, because most women are physically afraid of men they don't know. Men can hurt women, men can rape women, and if women are out having a drink, a too-large segment of society—some of whom might wind up on a jury—think it's the woman's own damn fault. Showcasing good intent is critical for a man establishing trust with a woman he's just met.

So, too, is actually *having* good intent. Research—lots and lots of it—has persistently shown that men overestimate women's sexual interest, perceiving behavior intended as mere politeness or even friendliness as potential friendliness-with-benefits.* So don't get aggressive if a woman whom you thought was sending you a signal turns out not to be. And so what if she's wearing a low-cut top and a miniskirt? She's not out there *being pretty at you*, she's just having a good time. And if her idea of a good time doesn't include your company, go find someone for whom it does.

Women, on their side, should stop expecting men to read their minds. You can make the first move, too, ladies. You can also let a man know when you're in the mood for sex, as well as when you're not, and exactly how big a deal you expect to be made of Valentine's Day, anniversaries, and the like. The women who most like to complain about men never listening tend to be the worst about actually communicating anything to the poor dears to begin with. Of course it would be lovely to have a partner so mystically attuned to one's needs and desires that no words are necessary. It would be lovely, too, to have a pony that never defecated. In the real world, we need to get in there with a

---

* Summing up this research, a report (entitled "Error Management Theory: A New Perspective on Biases in Cross-Sex Mind Reading") dryly notes, "Men's apparent error transcends the method used to study it." You can't make this stuff up.

shovel and clear things up from time to time. A good man won't find direct communication to be a mood killer; he'll find it a blessed relief.

Paying for the date

As a rule, the person who does the asking does the paying. The askee can contribute a tip, parking (which in some cities can run you more than dinner), or ice cream after the movie, if he *or* she wants. First dates shouldn't be excessively expensive, since the askee might feel awkward, and the asker resentful, if it turns out that the attraction is one-sided.

If the asker is a man, and your date insists on paying for half, let her. This insistence can give the impression of a rabid sort of feminism, but it's more likely the result of an overdeveloped sense of fair play, which isn't a bad quality in a girlfriend. (She'll probably expect you to cook, or at least clean up when she does, but she'll kill her own cockroaches. You could do worse.) It might also be the case that your date once had a nasty evening with a man less righteous than yourself who took it as a given that buying her dinner bought him rights to her affections for the evening. Most women have had more bad experiences than decent men can imagine, and this may lead to a certain amount of self-protective behavior on the first few dates. Work within her comfort zone and eventually you will *become* her comfort zone.

If the asker is a woman, and your date insists on paying for half—or all—of the evening, you and he might have slightly different ideas about gender equality. Or he just might not want to feel like a gigolo. People tend to want to present their best face on a first date, which means they often don't like to do unfamiliar things like eat strange food or participate in brand-new athletic activities. For a man, being asked out and having his dinner paid for by a woman is unfamiliar. So let him pick up his share of the bill if he feels awkward; it doesn't mean he's a chest-pounding Neanderthal, just that he wants to get back on familiar ground again. If he is a chest-pounding Neanderthal, you'll find that out on the second date.

And unless something horribly untoward happens, a second date is usually a good idea. Lots of people get performance anxiety around dating and don't show to their best advantage—or are so busy trying to make a good impression that they entirely forget to notice if their date is making a good impression on *them*. If the date was adequate but not magical, try another and see what happens.

Deflecting a pass

> **Question:** *Recently at a networking event I made good conversation with the people at my table, especially a nice man sitting next to me. He gave me his business card, but my husband later noticed that the man wrote his home address and phone number on the back of the card. I'm pretty sure I mentioned I'm married. Now I don't know if this man, who could be a good contact, was networking or looking for a date. Should I e-mail him or just move on?*

There are other reasons for men and women, even single men and women, to get together besides possible *luuuurve*. They might both be new in town and not know many other people, or have professional interests in common or hobbies that not a lot of other people they know share, or they may simply like each other in a nonromantic way. Opposite-sex friendships can be wonderful, but making the leap into them might involve an awkwardness that outstrips anything a first date has to offer.

If you've hit it off with an opposite-sex coworker or neighbor, the best way to get a friendship off the ground is to invite the person to group events with other friends, until you've socialized enough together that "Let's grab a beer after work on Friday" can't be misinterpreted—or at least is unlikely to be misinterpreted. It's a tricky situation. People need to realize that sometimes their expectations will be disappointed, that miscommunication will happen, and it's no one's fault. It's not because men are pigs or women are manipulative but because gender norms are in transition and we haven't worked out all the tricky bits yet. Sadly, there isn't any unmistakable yet ego-sparing way of making your platonic intentions clear.

That said, there are certain things you can do to lessen the chance of miscommunication.

- **Set friendly boundaries.** Keep any invitations limited to daytime activities that don't seem too date-like (no midnight salsa lessons). If it's the other person doing the asking, you could send the "not a date" message by saying, "Oh, I'd love to check out that new miniature golf course—my roommate and I were just talking about it. Shall I invite her along?"

- **Don't just say no.** Ask or accept an invitation when that's what you feel like doing—and don't pull back because you're worried you'll send the wrong message. Let your behavior on the outing make it clear whether it's a date. If you're on the receiving end of an unwanted pass, turn it down gently, appreciate the compliment, and move on. And if you're on the giving end of one, don't consider your time wasted—the person you asked out might become a friend and eventually introduce you to someone who *will* be interested romantically.

Sociologists who study networks have repeatedly found the value of "weak ties"—that is, acquaintanceships—in searches for jobs and romance. You see, you already know all of your close friends' single friends, so, as much as your friends love you, there isn't a great deal they can do for you. It's the people whose social worlds don't overlap with yours who can be the entrée to intriguing new possibilities in *lieben und arbeit*.

• **Hedge your bets.** Sometimes the person doing the asking isn't even clear about his or her own intentions. Maybe he hasn't quite decided how he feels about the askee; maybe the askee is a coworker or involved in a conflict of interest (for instance, a relative of a friend) that suggests the asker should tread very carefully. This is when it's time to deploy the plausible-deniability pass. The plausible-deniability pass is frequently spotted at professional events like networking parties and academic conferences, family events like weddings, and, for all I know, at Amish barn-raisings.

The plausible-deniability pass is a gesture by Party A that is subtle enough to allow Party B to choose how to interpret it: romantically if Party B is so inclined or non-romantically if Party B's interest is confined to business (or barn-raising).

If you are the target of a plausible-deniability pass and have no romantic interest in Party B, you can still take Party B up on future social and professional invitations. Even if you are married and suspect Party A of harboring illicit desires, you can still accept Party A's offer to buy you coffee sometime if you really want to pick Party A's brains about how to get sales up in the southwest region.

The plausible-deniability pass lacks the panache associated with great lovers of history and literature, like Cyrano de Bergerac, but the advantages are obvious in the business context, where swashbuckling soldier-poets are a bit de trop. Not only does it reduce the risk of rejection and awkwardness, but it also reflects the complexity of human relations. Party A might be looking for both business contacts *and* dates—there's no reason to assume it's either/or.

Defending your partner's honor

We don't fight duels anymore, but wise heterosexual folks know that they will occasionally have reason to defend a partner's honor when their same-sex friends rant or "joke" about the incompetence, incomprehensibility, or overall malignance of the opposite sex.

It can be difficult for people who are alone and who don't want to be alone, or who are in a relationship that is making them unhappy, to remind themselves that members of the opposite sex are *people*. After one too many frustrating Internet dates, it can be all to easy to see them as willfully obstinate obstacles to the emotional and physical intimacy you crave and deserve.

If you must rant to friends, keep the vitriol focused on individual situations—your lousy ex, your horrid blind date—and strive not to generalize your negativity to *all* men, *all* women, or *all* relationships. A good general rule is not to say anything about relationships or the opposite sex that you wouldn't want your partner to hear, if you're partnered, or that you wouldn't put in your personals ad, if you're not.

If a friend is ranting to you, acknowledge the pain but not the hate. Keep your responses focused on what he or she is feeling and the particulars of the situation; don't join in general man or woman bashing. If the conversation gets too extreme (as it can, for example, if you're hanging out with a group of the bitter and recently dumped), you might want to shut it down with, "I know you're hurt, but my wife is a woman/son is a man, and though I realize you're speaking more generally, I can't hear you talk about him/her like that." Ultimately, you'll be doing your friend a favor; people aren't likely to succeed in finding love when they've convinced themselves that all women are bitches or all men are bastards.

Treat nasty or demeaning jokes the same way you would treat a more overtly nasty statement, and don't let being accused of not having a sense of humor deter you. A good response to this attack is, "Clearly one of us is failing at humor, and I don't see any reason to assume it's me."

Romances: Other People's

Question: *I live on the second floor of an old three-family house with paper-thin walls. Sneezes and other everyday* *noise can be ignored. However, since a couple moved in above me, I have been woken by the sound of a bed banging against the wall. Once awake, I often hear other things I'd prefer not to hear. How might I suggest the couple consider rearranging their bedroom furniture and save all of us from embarrassment?*

In a perfect world, we would never be exposed to other people's cold germs, the smell of their cooking, the sight of their underwear, or the sound of their lovemaking. This is not the world we live in, especially if you live in a city with old buildings and thin walls. Decent people keep the evidence of their biological life as discreet as possible, but if a young urban couple has to stifle their cries of passion until they've saved up that 10 percent down payment, they may wind up spending the money on divorce attorneys rather than a starter home.

If you are hearing things you would rather not hear from your upstairs neighbors' love nest, you might want to get to know your neighbors and see if a direct approach might work (somewhat) comfortably. There are certainly folks whose response to being told that their lovemaking is entertaining the entire condo would be to laugh uproariously and then find creative ways for quieting their sex lives. You might all become lifelong friends, eventually summering in Florida together during your sunset-and-Viagra years and reminiscing about the passion and paper-thin walls of your youth. If the notion of speaking directly to your neighbors makes you vaporish, try a musical experiment. When you're awakened by their passion, turn on the radio, loud enough to be audible upstairs. Turn it off when the noise stops. After you've done this a few times, they'll get the message, but the medium is indirect enough that no one need be embarrassed.*

If you are *seeing* things you'd rather not, move on. Seeing things you don't want to is one of the risks you take when you leave the house. If friends are engaging in heavy PDA and moving on is not an option, speak to whomever of the couple you're closest to and voice your discomfort. Alternately, you could take an aggressively comic approach. Nothing withers the romantic impulse quite like a well-timed quip. Convey the message that their behavior is silly (not "transgressive" or refreshingly open), and they might well stop. I'm sure you have your own comic style, but I'm tempted myself to drop into sportscaster mode and narrate the action:

> And they kiss! His hand is creeping up into her hair—was that a little tug there? It was! He's going for the Stanley Kowalski he-man approach this time, and it looks like she's responding to it! Whoops, her right hand's going below the table line. Can't see the action now but it looks like they both brought their "A" game today, folks!

They'll think you're obnoxious and immature, but you already think that of them, so what's the harm?

How to be a good coupled friend

What's the biggest fault line in society, sex- and genderwise? Maybe it's men versus women, or straights versus gays, or feminists versus traditionalists—but a good argument can be made that it's couples versus singles. What makes this fault line

---

* Wait, wait, I've got it: when that bed starts a-rockin', it's time to put some Bach in. Or maybe not.

different from the others is that most of us will spend a significant amount of our lives in both camps. You'd think this would make it easier, but it doesn't seem to do so. To be a good coupled friend:

- **Be available.** The main thing partnered folks owe singletons is *time*. It's natural enough in the first glow of new love to neglect your friends a bit, and frankly they may find your absence preferable to having every social occasion hijacked by your soliloquies about the great and glorious amour you have found. (I'm all for patience with those who are in the obsessive early stages of parenthood, graduate school, addiction recovery, religious conversion, book writing—ahem—and other identity-changing pursuits, but there's no ignoring the fact that it *is* irritating.) But after the first couple of months, your social life ought to get back to normal. It's rotten to make your friends feel that they were stopgap measures, sad substitutes for romantic love. And you'll want them to reality-check you about the appropriateness of that new love and to comfort you if the new love wasn't as true as you'd hoped. Any love, new or old, who works to separate you from your friends is bad news.

- **Appreciate that being single can be a choice.** If your friends say they are happy being single, believe them. Not everyone is meant for marriage, and even those who are go through periods when single life feels right and healthy to them. Don't treat them as though they're putting up a wonderfully brave front or offer to set them up on blind dates.

- **Make matches with care.** If your friends aren't happy being single, you still want to put care into setting them up on blind dates. If the date in question is manifestly unsuitable—an atheist for the devout Catholic, an SUV lover for the environmentalist—you are, in essence, telling your friend, "You're obviously so desperate I'm assuming you'll take anything at this point." Sexual attraction and psychological compatibility are mighty complex things— think of some of the couples you know, and ask yourself if it ever would have occurred to you to set them up if you'd known them in their single days—so don't paralyze yourself with second-guessing. But do be able to list at least a few attributes that you think might lead to compatibility beyond the appropriate genitalia ("You both love the outdoors and gardening," "He grew up in California and practices yoga, too," and so on).

- **Understand that being single takes time.** Your single friends may or may not have large apartments to clean up or children to ferry to soccer practice, and they don't have a spouse who needs time and attention. But they also don't have someone to help them dig their cars out of the snow in the winter, take their cats to the vet, get them orange juice and NyQuil when they have colds, or pay the bills if they lose their job. They have almost all the same responsibilities as married people do, and it all falls on their shoulders. This can be frightening at times and wearying at others. Often, partnered people like to glamorize the lives of singletons as an endless round of shoe stores and sports bars and open horizons. Be more respectful of your single friends than to project your own fantasies and regrets on them.

- **Make chore dates.** For the happily partnered, "doing chores" and "hanging out" overlap a lot. It's fun to make dinner together, to spend a sunny Saturday running errands and washing the car, to shop for a new throw rug for the bathroom. Single people like to do these things together, too. So when you're planning social time, don't think only in terms of Officially Fun activities like going to movies, bowling, or eating out. Your single friends might also like some company doing the mundane chores that have to be done.

- **Keep your friends' secrets** if you're asked to, even from your significant other.

How to be a good single friend

To be a good single friend to a couple (whether you originally met them as a couple or a friend has paired up):

- **Get to know a couple as *individuals*.** Keep in mind that these two people may hold different political or religious beliefs and enjoy different activities. You don't have to nurture equally strong relationships with both of them or always suggest activities that both enjoy. If Tiffany likes to ride horses and Calvin likes to play computer games and you like to do both, ride with Tiffany and Wii away with Calvin. (This goes for couples who are friends with couples, too. In some parts of the country and in certain subcultures it's not considered appropriate to socialize with an opposite-sex married friend, but if that's okay in your world, do it.)

• **Humanize your friends' partners.** If a friend of yours becomes coupled, treat the new significant other as a person in his or her own right, not as your friend's most excellent new piece of sporting equipment.

• **Don't consider yourself a plus one.** Don't feel self-conscious about being a third wheel or any sort of odd-numbered appendage. The Noah's Ark days of hostesses frantically searching for an extra man are over, thank God. Socialize with your coupled friends and don't worry about occasionally being the lone singleton in a group of couples. If you've been invited, it's because people enjoy your company, not because they feel sorry for you. (If you are recently bereaved of your significant other, you might not want to socialize with other couples for a while, and this is understandable. In general, though, singletons ought to get out there.)

• **Consider the (potential) wedding toast.** Dating stories are great, and married friends love to hear them—the longer they've been married, in fact, the more they enjoy hearing your adventures. Keep in mind, though, that someday you might get permanent with one of these dates. Don't tell anything that you wouldn't want to have running through your friends' minds at the wedding. And while your friends should keep your secrets, even from their own spouses or sweeties, it's safest to assume that the spouse-sweetie is told everything unless you've specifically asked your friend not to.

Just as you want to be seen as yourself and not as a stunted frat jock living an endless round of ESPN and booty calls, or as a cat collector nursing chamomile tea and philodendrons, don't stereotype your married friends. Don't treat them like the psychic equivalent of Mom and Dad, or assume that they're never lonely or that they can't possibly know what the stresses of single life are like. For once in our lives, at least, we've *all* been there.

· 5 ·

Mother, May I?

CHILDREN

"All happy families are alike; every unhappy family is
unhappy in its own way."   —Leo Tolstoy

Does anyone have as much to answer for as Leo Tolstoy (or his PR rep) when it comes to our twisted ideas
of family life? This opening line, arguably the most quoted "parenting" wisdom in literature, promotes a fear-mongering
judgmentalism—the idea that there's a right way to run your
family life and then unlimited numbers of wrong ways, all of
which should be dissected with vicious and tragic abandon.

What a horrible way to live! There are as many right ways
of being in a family as there are families—and individuals.
You'll live longer and be happier if you take as your own the
philosophy of the great Persian rug weavers: that no matter
how beautiful and complex a pattern you are weaving, you
must be sure always to make at least one mistake, because perfection belongs only to God. If that's a bit too mystical for you,
try on this wise, compassionate, and true-to-real-life quote

from David Byrne of Talking Heads: "There's a million ways to get things done, there's a million ways to make things work out."

Throughout the millennia and across cultures, there has been extraordinary variety in human child-rearing practices. Not all of them are equally good, of course. Yet it's safe to say that parents can choose from quite a few equally adaptive ways to bring up kids. There's no one perfect method, and no point in looking for the "natural" way to raise a child. Even research on modern-day primitive tribes shows a large variation in attitudes about and behavior toward children. Children can, and do, thrive under many different kinds of circumstances.

Parents, however, thrive under exactly one kind of circumstance: being supported and honored in the hard work they are doing. Our culture does a horrible job at this, all while driving up the standards for what it takes to be a "good" parent. The modern ideal of an intensive cultivation of children that requires 100 percent, 24/7 parenting is a very new one; even in the 1950s, a decade extolled for its traditional family values, children were thought to develop most healthily given a fair amount of benign neglect on the part of their parents. The Cleavers might have eaten dinner together every night, but Beaver and Wally had plenty of time to noodle around on their own without adult supervision or the necessity of ensuring that every single one of their activities promoted their physical, social, or intellectual development. Our expectations for parents these days are a good deal more freighted. Still, the minute parents actually internalize those expectations, we shriek, "Helicopter parent! Bad Mommy! Bad Daddy!" at them. There's no winning.

This chapter is premised on two interdependent principles:

- Kids are resilient, and
- Parents are people.

Believing that parents are people means believing that mothers and fathers are entitled to basic human rights and respect. This includes, among other things, respect for their bodily autonomy and decision-making competence, privacy, access to public space, and appreciation and support for raising the generation on which we'll depend—all of which they're highly unlikely to get from their kids, mind you, which makes it even more crucial that the rest of us give them a hand.

Life B.C. —Before Children

That nice couple down the street who would make such terrific parents—they're so energetic and fun, they have that great yard and plant a vegetable garden every summer, which would be so educational for children to work on—you're just dying to know if they plan to have kids. Should you ask? Your college friend who always spoke as though she planned to have children but has now been married for five years with none on the way—do you say anything?

Some people would say no, never, not under any circumstances, it's *just too personal*. This seems ridiculously uptight. Just because someone asks if you are going to have children doesn't mean they're preaching that you should, after all. But these questions need to be handled carefully. Never assume that a couple plans to have children. No "Enjoy your ballroom dance lessons now; you won't have time when the kids come" unless the as-yet-nonexistent kids are publicly announced to be on their way imminently. And don't ask about the childbearing plans of acquaintances or colleagues whom you don't know well. A couple may be happily childless by choice—or they may be struggling with infertility, one of life's great sources of pain. Or perhaps one member of the couple wants children and the other one remains uncertain. (And don't be too sure which one it is! Contrary to stereotype, women of childbearing age today tend to have more positive attitudes toward childlessness and report less belief that children are essential for happiness and meaning than women did some forty years ago.) Or perhaps both want kids, but they can't afford it yet and are in a desperate race of economics against biology. Are these really the kind of struggles you want to bring up in order to satisfy casual curiosity? Of course they aren't. So don't ask.

When it's a good friend, however, I don't see that asking "Do you plan/want to have children?" is any more of an invasion of privacy than asking, "Do you believe in God?" or "Do you think you'll stay with this career for the rest of your life?" or "What's the most embarrassing thing you've ever done?" Which is to say, of *course* they're invasions of privacy! What else are friends for if not to invade our privacy? You want isolation, go live on a mountaintop. Down here in the valley, we're all about community. Look at it this way: if you're close enough to the person that you might someday get asked to babysit, it is your business. (I give short shrift, also, to unmarried couples who say that "it's nobody's business" to ask if they plan to marry or not. If you're going to be expecting wedding presents someday, then you've made it their business, haven't you?)

But as with all questions, there are ways to ask and ways not to. The guidelines below are, obviously, intended for popping the "Do you plan to have kids?" question, but many can be adapted to other dicey personal queries as well.

- **Realize that they may feel pressured.** The acceptability of asking about a couple's reproductive plans varies in inverse proportion to how long they have been married.* It's one thing to ask people if they plan to have kids when they're just engaged or recently married, as it's unlikely, at that point, for the issue to be a sore spot. A couple who's been married for five years or more, however, either doesn't want them or can't have them, and might just as soon not be asked.

  And for heaven's sake never ask an older childless couple if they wished they had had children. You'll have no one to blame but yourself if their response is, "Not if they'd turned out like you."

- **Phrase the question as neutrally as possible.** I can't help but be offended when people ask if Mr. Improbable and I "have a family." No, we have no family, we achieved sentience miraculously when lightning hit a patch of slime mold. Of course we have family, parents and extended family, and they most certainly count. Furthermore, as far as the two of us are concerned, we don't think of family as something we *have*, we think of it as something we *are*. It's better to say "children" than family and "do you plan"

---

* Yes, single people, unmarried couples, and gay couples who can't yet legally marry also have children. But partly *because* these people face special societal challenges to having kids, they don't get nudged incessantly about whether and when they're going to take the plunge, as though children were a refreshing glass of instant iced tea.

rather than "do you hope/want"—they might indeed hope or want but be stymied. If you're not sure how to ask, preface your question with that fact: "I hope you don't mind my asking, and I hope I ask this in a way that keeps you comfortable." (Though any question requiring so many qualifiers may be better left unasked.)

- **Build an "escape clause" into your question.** By building a vague but positively tilted option into the question, you allow people to both be honest and maintain their privacy. For instance, "Do you plan to have children, or are you happy with it just being the two of you?" This is a good technique for any intimate questions ("Do you plan to get married, or do you figure if it ain't broke, don't fix it?") as well as requests for favors that people might feel awkward refusing ("Can you serve on the auction committee this year, or are you already overcommitted?" or "May I bring my new significant other to your dinner party, or do you need to keep the guest list down?") Before long, escape clauses will become such an automatic habit that you'll find yourself asking, "Honey, do you want another cup of coffee, or should I go soak my head?"

- **Whatever answer you receive, accept it.** Especially when it comes to child having and raising, others will make decisions you may never understand. Parents may find it hard to understand how a life without children can be meaningful. Those who don't much like kids may be flabbergasted when a similarly indifferent friend makes the extraordinary leap of faith to have her own. Among parents, especially mothers, some cannot comprehend how a woman could go out to work and leave her children in day care; others cannot imagine having children and then being unable to support them financially. When someone's deep, existential choices don't in any way accord with how you make sense of the universe, let it go. Prying and prodding will never make it clear to you, it will just alienate the other person and leave her feeling judged and wanting.

Sometimes, of course, you don't need to ask if someone plans to have a child because they're gestating or nursing one right there in front of you.

Bellies and Breasts and Bottles, Oh My

"You should never say anything to a woman that even re-motely suggests you think she's pregnant unless you can see an actual baby emerging from her at that moment."

—Dave Barry

Yes, this advice is probably in every etiquette book under the sun . . . but, knowing better, I've still actually *done* this, and I can vouch for what a purely awful experience it is. "And you're having a second, how wonderful!" I enthused when I bumped baskets with her in the aisle of the health-food store. "Nope, just haven't lost the weight from the first," she replied flatly, turning to a bin of bitter herbs.* Then I died of embarrassment and turned into slime mold and waited for the lightning to reanimate me.

Another taboo: You don't *pet* pregnant women or treat them as though their bodies have suddenly become public property.

---

* To this day, the scents of cardamom and chamomile make me shudder.

They are sharing their bodies with their babies, not with you. So no comments or questions on diet, safety-belt wearing, pre-school choosing, doulas versus doctors, or anything else unless the pregnant woman herself opens the conversation. Have you ever seen a pregnant woman wearing a T-shirt that said, "Please give me unsolicited advice and tell me your birthing horror stories"? Neither have I. So don't act as though their protruding bellies are sending the same message. And if you are a pregnant woman, feel free to shut down unwelcome touches or comments firmly, without snark or apology. You'll need a good "because I'm the mom" authority voice when the kid comes anyway, so you may as well start practicing it.

Another land mine of expecting is the issue of breast-feeding in public. Although Americans are generally pro-breast-feeding, most of them don't want to see it. I admit that public breast-feeding is something I'm uncomfortable about, myself—but I've also decided that my discomfort doesn't matter *squat*. It's just an irrational reaction against something unfamiliar that will fade with time. Or it won't. The point is, it's my problem, not the breast-feeding mother's. As with physical displays of affection or political bumper stickers, when you leave the house, you might see things that make you uncomfortable. There's an easy solution: don't look.

A common objection to public nursing is, "Just because it's natural, doesn't mean it should be public," with a few hot-air references to other biological activities that ought not be done out in the open thrown in for punctuation. This is ridiculous. *Nursing is not the same as those other biological activities because it is hygienic.*

It is also necessary. When a woman has chosen nursing there's no "off" switch—she needs to nurse regularly, just as her baby needs to be nursed. So not allowing breast-feeding in public effectively bars women and babies from public space—not exactly a triumph for women's or children's rights. If we can all agree that infants have the right to eat and that mothers have the right to leave the house, the logical conclusion is that nursing in public should be accepted.* As for modesty—please. An infant's head covers more of a woman's breast than plenty of current fashions do.

One of the things that made me rethink my knee-jerk discomfort was the day it dawned on me that about half the time I didn't even notice a woman was breast-feeding. There was just this swirl of cardigan and baby and blankets and whatnot going on down there.

Finally, *not* breast-feeding—in public or anywhere else—is all right, too. There's entirely too much self-righteousness and bullying that "breast is best," which can make women who can't breast-feed feel downright rotten. So if you see a woman bottle-feeding her baby, as long as the bottle isn't marked "Smirnoff," assume she's doing the best she can and shut up.

Mannerly without Children

> "There are essentially two classes in America: not rich and poor, and not even black and white, and certainly not Anglo and Hispanic, but those who have younger children and those who do not."   —Alan Wolfe

It's not necessary to like children in order to be a polite childless person. Occasionally, I've heard the argument that saying you dislike children is as morally repugnant as saying you dislike

---

* And an infant with a breast in its mouth is an infant who isn't screaming!

black people or gays, but this is extremely faulty logic. Children are cognitively different from adults, in qualitative and predictable ways that some people are going to find delightful and surprising and others will find tedious beyond measure. There's no reason to be militant about the tedium, however. Whom are you trying to convince? Do you really think that a mother of three is going to say, "Jeepers, you're right! They *are* disgusting little rug rats! I'm so embarrassed. I can't imagine what I must have been thinking. Do you think Angelina Jolie might want them, or should I just put them up for offer on Craigslist?" The children you find so annoying to hear about may someday be your oncologist, mutual-fund manager, or nursing-home administrator. What kind of world do you want to be living in when you're old and vulnerable? All of us—not just parents—are invested in the next generation. Other people's children are going to create that world, so be nice to them now. (And don't complain about your taxes paying for public schools that you're not using: you will get, if you aren't already getting, the benefit of good schools—just indirectly.)

What do you do with children? Some childless people adore them; some dislike them; some are charmed but bewildered. Randall Jarrell has a wonderful description of the mentality of someone who dislikes children in his academic satire *Pictures from an Institution*:

> This was what Gertrude didn't like about children: they didn't act like grown-ups. She couldn't understand why they didn't act more like grown-ups—a little more like, anyway; it seemed to her almost affectation on their part. . . . Children not only bored her, she felt that she was right to be bored by them. The double standard that people employ for children and grown-ups seemed to her

a grotesquely disproportionate one. . . . . What can you *talk*
to children about, Gertrude thought despairingly.

It's fine to arrange your life primarily along adults-only lines
if you're a Gertrude type.

- **Being polite to young children.** When children are
  unavoidable, however, this is what you do: you talk to
  them about their *stuff*. Ask them to show you their stuff
  and they're yours. (This works with adults, too, of course:
  "Ooh, an iPhone! Can you show me how it works?") Better
  yet, don't bother *talking* to children at all, which Gertrude
  never figured out. *Do* things with them instead. Learn a
  couple of nifty tricks you can teach them: juggling, making
  cookies, an art or science project. Children also like to
  dance, and they will be impressed by even your most
  pathetic moves, so they're great partners on the dance
  floor (or living room carpet).

- **Being polite to tweens, teens, and young adults.** You *do*
  talk to teenagers, although the conversation works best if
  you mostly just listen. Honestly, given the grilling some
  high school– and college-aged folks are subjected to, I'd
  fully understand if they countered with, "Saving enough for
  retirement these days? You're not getting any younger" or "I
  was reading an article last week about the dwindling
  economic security of the middle class—are you keeping up
  on continuing education in your field? It's tough out there
  in the real world!" (Before anyone leaps in to decry the
  narcissism of today's youth and how we shouldn't
  contribute to it by being polite to them, ask yourself, how

are teenagers supposed to learn good conversational skills if the only conversational strategies they're exposed to are unsolicited advice, judgmentalism, and prying?)

You can bring up the college and postcollege plans if you demonstrate that you don't want to lecture them but want to hear what they have to say, instead. This is an immensely stressful time of life, with many details to keep track of, many choices, and much (or so it seems) riding on the balance. In other words, try "Gosh it's so hard"/"How are you coping?" rather than "Are you doing the right things?"/"This is the easiest time of your life"/"Wait till you get out in the real world, kid." (Which approach would *you* rather someone take when asking about a stressful situation?) Discussing hobbies, music, and pop culture can be easy even if you don't know the band, book, TV show, or fashion trend under discussion. Pretend you are talking to a witty and accomplished foreigner explaining the customs and art of his country, and ask questions.

• **Being polite to the parents.** For childless people, alas, most of the problems come from parents. Childless folks should take no guff from those who have reproduced, if such guff is proffered—either of the "you'll change your mind" variety or the "moral superiority" variety. The best response to "Oh, you'll change your mind," is "That's a profoundly disrespectful thing to say about another person's life choices" in as flat and unemotional a tone as you can manage. If you're accused of selfishness for not wanting children, you can always ask why the accuser thinks it would be a *good* thing for selfish people to have children. My favorite one-two punch has always been people who accuse you of selfishness for not having children, and then in the next breath ask if you aren't worried about having someone to take care of you when you're old. Apparently viewing another human being as a 401(k) plan on legs doesn't strike them as self-serving.

People can have kids for selfish, narcissistic reasons, and they can stay childless for selfish, narcissistic reasons, too. You can have children because it's easier to just cave in to family pressure to do so; in the hopes that someone will love you unconditionally; in order to fit in socially; or because you never got to be the football hero or homecoming queen and want to bask in your child's reflected glory. Or you can stay childless because you want to keep your tight abs. None of these are particularly good reasons, but the difference is, staying childless for the wrong reasons doesn't embroil an innocent human life in your narcissism. If your reasons for not having kids are shallow and immature, cling to them all the harder.

Finally, one area where there should be no division between parents and nonparents: work-life balance. Pitting moms and dads who leave early to coach Jaden's soccer game against singletons or childless folks who work late is a divide-and-conquer tactic benefiting neither side. *Everyone* should get adequate time off to care for their physical and emotional health and that of the people in their lives. If parents get to leave early to take care of a sick child, but you don't get to leave early because your elderly mother needs someone to take her to the doctor, don't bitch at the mommies—get together with them and approach management as a united front. Clever parents are very, very good about presenting a united front; you want the parenthood-honed negotiation skills on your side for this one.

Mannerly with Children

The major thing that parents owe childless people—and other parents and the rest of the world and, most especially, their own children—is bringing up children who develop good social skills, understand how to deal with a variety of social situations and people, and know that they are not the center of the universe. This doesn't happen overnight (most people don't really seem to reach this point of self-awareness until they're forty), and as long as you're clearly making your children's social skills a work in progress, you have the right to be cut some slack. No one learns social skills in a vacuum, and children, like everyone, need to fail sometimes in order to learn.

- **Teach your kids good manners.** Kids *want* to learn good manners, because they have that natural human desire to want to be able to predict and control the world around them. Children who know that they can say and do the right thing are children who are comfortable in their own skin—and comfortable improvising when "the rules" don't seem to be sufficient. It's sad to see kids whose parents haven't taught them social basics; other people, both adults and children, don't respond well to them and the kids can't figure out why. You're not trammeling a noble savage by teaching your kids manners; humans exist in a social world, constituted by our relationships with others, and good manners help children find their bearings. It's helpful to present social skills in an empowering, rather than punitive, way. Give your kids the sense that they are learning skills that will make their lives easier and more fun, skills that will enable them to do *more* in the world, rather than less. For example, children should start writing thank-you notes as soon as they're old enough to open their own gifts. Even before they're able to write, they can draw or make handprints—and if you make it a fun crafts project, rather than a dreary chore, they'll get into the habit.

- **Realize that not everyone will delight in your kids like you do.** No matter how socially adept your children are, not everyone is going to find them delightful, and the reasonable parent understands that. There are some people in the world who simply don't enjoy the company of children, and there's little use in trying to convert them. Foisting your child upon them—either in the flesh or in the form of endless stories—is likely only to solidify their dislike and possibly expand it from a dislike of children to their parents. Never ask someone to hold your baby unless they have either asked or clearly indicated through enthusiastic clucking and cooing that they do, indeed, want to. (Parents are particularly prone to do this to grandmother-aged women, or so I am told. Not every senior lady wants to be a grandma, and even those who do may prefer to reserve the coos and clucks for their own grandchildren.)

- **Realize that some things are for grown-ups.** Another faux pas that constantly creeps into Miss Conduct's mailbox: whether to bring uninvited children to parties, weddings, funerals, and other grown-up events. If your children are not specifically invited (either by name or by "Kids welcome"), do not bring them. And don't ask, because by doing so you put the host in an awkward position. Everyone, even the most devoted parents, needs adult time to refresh their conversational skills and remind themselves of what it is they're trying to raise their children *into*—informed, interesting, engaged adults.

Of course, not all childless folks dislike children, not even those who are childless by choice. Be patient with people who are well-meaning but awkward with children. We live in a time of near-unprecedented age segregation. According to two Norwegian professors, Gunhild O. Hagestad and Peter Uhlenberg, who study the issue, "It can be argued that in today's Western societies, the family represents the only true age integrated social institution." Nonparents often don't get much practice dealing with kids, and children don't get much practice dealing with adults who are not related to them or paid to care for them. So don't get huffy with friends or acquaintances who aren't child-literate—they may simply not have had the chance to learn. Be prepared to scaffold interactions and coach both kids and adults in mutually supportive and enjoyable activities.

Different Kinds of Parents, Part One
Parenting Styles

Question: *During a casual conversation, my brother-in-law asked how I felt about toy guns for my two-year-old daughter. I told him I felt pretty strongly that toy guns*

were inappropriate for toddlers and didn't want her play-
ing with them. For Christmas, he gave her several toy
guns and informed me he thought my viewpoint was dumb
and that he was "overriding" it. I didn't want to start a
family feud just then, but is it appropriate for me to tell
him not to do that again?

You Ferberize, and I practice attachment parenting. Who's right? I say Barbie is a tool of the patriarchy, you say she's a harmless template onto which girls project their own ambitions and dreams. Who's right? You're organic all the way, I say let the kid have the occasional Twinkie so she doesn't develop an eating disorder. Who's right?

I can't answer those questions definitively—but I can certainly warn you away from anyone who tries to. My doctorate is in developmental psychology, and if it taught me anything, it's to beware of headlines heralding some new finding about the psychology of children's development. In fact, you might just want to declare a moratorium on watching the Discovery Channel or reading the *New York Times* health pages from now until your child has, say, gone through menopause—and then only if she hasn't produced any grandchildren for you to worry over.

Why shouldn't these studies be taken too seriously? Aren't they *science?* Well, yes. But there are three main reasons for skepticism about anything you hear reported in the news:

1. The things that matter are hard to measure. How happy a child is, how healthy the child's relationship with her parents and peers, even how intelligent a child is—these things are impossible to measure. All scientists can measure are epiphenomena and proxy numbers like self-

reports, serotonin levels, and IQ scores. We can't measure things like happiness or intelligence—we can only measure the signs of them.* And it is no wonder that every few years some major debate breaks out about whether a given sign is "really" measuring the thing we're trying to at all.

2. You can't randomly assign parents into groups. The hallmark of science is random assignment, which means, say, you sort half the rats randomly into one group and half into another, give one half the smart drugs and the other half the placebos (without even telling the lab assistants which half is which), and then see which of the rats learn the maze fastest. Clearly, differences in parenting styles can't be assessed like that. "All right, you lot, you nurse until age two—you over there, wean 'em at six months." Since it's unethical to treat people like lab rats, this means that we can look only at naturally occurring parental behaviors, and generally good parenting behaviors tend to clump together, just as generally bad ones do.

3. The importance of good fits, innate risks, and benefit factors. Kids aren't blank slates. They're born with personalities and temperaments, and what works with one kid—as any parent with more than one can testify—often doesn't work with another. Some kids bounce back immediately from a spanking; others brood for days over a cross glance. Some thrive on intellectual structure; some need time to just noodle around and figure things

---

* Jerome Lettvin, a great MIT neurologist, psychiatrist, and electrical engineer—someone who really ought to know, in other words—once said, "Science consists of measuring with great precision that which does not matter."

out for themselves. Kids also vary enormously in terms of how resilient they are. We all know people who survived neglect or even abuse and came out of it loving and centered, and people who are still coping with the effects of what may seem on the surface to have been very minor setbacks in childhood.

This doesn't mean that developmental psychology, or studies about the effects of various educational, nutritional, and disciplinary practices on children, are pointless. When scientists look at a large number of studies conducted in different communities over a long period of time, they can see what the trends are—and recommend policies that will work well for most children most of the time. But are you raising most children most of the time? It may feel like that some days, but I doubt it's actually the case. You're raising only your own kids, and you have to trust your instincts on what works best for them and for you.

Most newspapers, magazines, and TV shows aren't reporting on these kinds of large-scale meta-analyses (the practice of looking at lots of studies at once to see what conclusions can be drawn—it's statistically very complicated but the best way of figuring out what's really going on). Your average newspaper article reports the results of a single study, often conducted on a small number of subjects, and it may not even report the results accurately. Most reporters aren't trained to interpret statistics; they are trained to simplify and (sometimes) sensationalize.*

So don't torture yourself over the latest findings that making

---

* A popular exercise in psychology classes is to have students look up a newspaper report on a study, and then look up the study itself and see how accurately it was reported. This results in some mighty media-skeptical students, I tell you what.

your kid eat broccoli when he hates it will turn him into a serial killer, while a deficiency of green vegetables in his diet will lower his IQ. The most important things children need are consistency, attention, and love, and *you know that*. Children are resilient. Don't worry about the small things, like broccoli and Barbies and Baby Mozart; be whatever kind of parent you are, and let other parents be what kind they are, too. Sure, your children might well end up in therapy someday complaining about all the mistakes you made. But chances are they'll wind up there, or not, no matter what you did (assuming you were a good enough parent to begin with). And whatever mistakes you're worried about today aren't the ones they'll be carping to Dr. Schadenfreude about in twenty years, so cut yourself some slack.

And don't give other parents grief about their parenting styles or take any grief from others about yours. Direct criticism can be addressed with a straightforward, "I'm not interested in criticism of how I raise my children, thank you." Passive-aggressive one-upmanship is a trickier thing to deal with. Don't play into hyper-competitive parents' games—either by one-upping them with your own child's accomplishments or with snarky comments like, "I'm so glad we've decided to relax and just let Caitlin be a child." Instead, react much as you do to your child when she is going through that inevitable "Hey, watch me!" stage: just keep repeating, in a warm yet bored voice, "Wow, that's great. Wow, that's great. I'm so proud of you. Wow, that's great." The message will get through, and even if it doesn't, you'll have amused yourself.

But even without competition, different parenting styles can lead to problems.

- **Agree on rules in advance.** Parents with different styles should communicate in advance about policies and rules when kids and/or adults are spending time together. It's tough to discipline another person's kid, unless safety is at stake or you've had clear-cut rules-setting discussions with the parents in advance. Chances are good you'll wind up mostly socializing with folks whose parenting styles are similar to your own—differences in parenting styles usually reflect deep underlying philosophical and political differences. Still, even the most compatible parents will have different hot-button issues, from television to refined sugar to the importance of saying "May I be excused?" So when you're talking, keep your comments focused on specific behaviors: "We're working on 'Please,' so please don't give Amanda anything unless she says the magic word." This keeps your explanations clear and your tone nonjudgmental.

What you don't want to do—if you want to keep the relationship intact—is to get dragged into a debate about child-raising philosophy. And think through in advance where you might be willing to compromise. A mother of my acquaintance noted that she will give way on sweets occasionally, since the worst consequence is a mild tummy ache, but that bedtime is sacrosanct, because everyone suffers the next day if her son doesn't get enough sleep.

- **Hold guests to your house rules.** You can certainly enforce "house rules" to protect yourself and your own family and property, just as you would in dealing with an adult. It's perfectly acceptable to have a "no profanity" or "no touching the dog" rule in the house, and to let people (of any age) know that if they can't abide by those rules, they needn't consider themselves your guests anymore.

If another person—whether a parent or not—deliberately undermines your house policies, stand up for yourself and your parenting style. The old saying, "Fool me once, shame on you; fool me twice, shame on me," might be cold comfort, but it's a good rule of thumb for gearing yourself up to deal with disorderly grown-ups. If you've clearly stated that you don't believe toy guns are appropriate for your daughter, for example, it would be appropriate to return the gift with a note saying something along the lines of, "Thank you, but we do not want our daughter to have toy guns and would appreciate it if you would respect our wishes in the future. Happy New Year!"

When standing up to a relative, particularly grandparents, be sure to talk first to your significant other or ex about how to handle the situation. Unilaterally taking on in-laws is a double mistake: to ignore your spouse's feelings is a breach of your relationship, and to ignore your spouse's combat advice is a strategic error.

Different Kinds of Parents, Part Two: The Mommy Wars

The mainstream media love the story of the mommy wars: stay-at-home mothers versus mothers who work. And any time the media are spinning a story as a catfight—stay-at-home moms versus working moms, second-wave feminists versus Gen Y "postfeminists"—you can think of it as a flare, warning you about an underlying structural problem. It's easier, and more comfortable, for the media to retreat to that mythical narrative about how women are always one step away from clawing one another's eyes out: no need for statistics, no deep reporting, no deep thinking about what this means for society.

And there are serious social problems. As a species, we are what is known as "cooperative breeders." In cooperative-breeder species, the mother alone cannot care for the offspring while simultaneously keeping herself fed; she needs help from her mate or other members of her group. Day care, in other words, is not the invention of 1970s feminism; it's found among honeybees, scrub jays, wolves, marmosets, and plenty of modern-day hunter-gatherer tribes, to name just a few.

Yet in the United States today, we've settled into a general societal consensus that places having children into a category closer to a hobby than a job or social good, and like all hobbies the cost should be borne entirely by the people who choose to take it up. A recent survey of 177 countries revealed that 168 of them offered guaranteed leave with income to mothers, with 98 offering fourteen weeks or more off work. Among the minority that did not: Lesotho, Liberia, Papua New Guinea, Swaziland—and the United States. Countries around the globe support their cooperative breeders:

- 107 countries "protect working women's right to breast-feed"
- 137 require paid vacations annually
- 134 have a maximum workweek length
- 126 have mandatory days off each week
- 145 mandate sick days

Sadly, the United States does not have a national mandate on even one of these issues.

When combined with the basic facts of Americans' work values and schedules, the lack of work-life balance programs has a devastating effect. Mothers who want to work are faced with juggling a presumed 100 percent, 24/7 commitment to the workplace as well as a self-imposed (or peer-pressured) 100 percent, 24/7 commitment to parenthood. The past few decades have seen increasing work hours—from mandatory overtime for blue-collar and service workers to expected fifty-plus-hour weeks for professionals. And there's little between those two ends of the spectrum; good part-time, or even thirty-five- to forty-hours-a-week, jobs that offer benefits and opportunities for promotion are increasingly rare. Multiple surveys have found that both men and women want to spend more time with families and are willing to sacrifice *some* money and status to do so—but not their entire careers. Unfortunately, they're rarely able to get what they want.

But stories in the media about women who stay home rather than work—the *New York Times* has been doing semiannual versions of this story since the 1950s, according to scholars at the Center for WorkLife Law at the University of California, Hastings—nearly always frame the issue as one of personal choice. Is it really? As E. J. Graff, the coauthor of *Getting Even: Why Women Don't Get Paid Like Men—and What to Do About It*, wrote:

> "Choice" is emphasized in eighty-eight of the 119 articles [Joan C. Williams] surveyed. But keep reading. Soon you find that staying home wasn't these women's first choice, or even their second. Rather, every other door slammed. . . . More than a third of the articles in Williams's report cite "workplace inflexibility" as a reason mothers leave their jobs. . . . Only by ignoring both the women's own stories and the larger context can these moms-go-home articles

keep chirping on about choice and how these women now
have "the best job in the world."

The repeated talk of "choice" makes women feel entirely responsible for the situations they find themselves in. Is a mother
who works full-time really making a "choice" if she dare not
even ask for a reduction in hours because her husband is self-
employed and she provides the family's health insurance? Is a
stay-at-home mother really making a "choice" if the public
schools are so bad that they must be supplemented or replaced
by homeschooling, or if child care would cost more than she
can earn? If we label the decision to stay home versus to go off
to work as a "choice," it allows us, as a society, to maintain that
any negative consequences are a problem for the individual to
solve, and don't require reform of our laws or workplace cultures.

I'm not here to offer policy recommendations—only the
politeness recommendations that both working and stay-at-home
mothers recognize that the other side, like they themselves, are
making decisions under severely difficult circumstances. Women
who leave the workplace find it extraordinarily hard to get back
in, according to a *Harvard Business Review* article by Sylvia Ann
Hewlett and Carolyn Buck Luce: only 40 percent of highly qualified professional women who take time out manage to return to
full-time professional work, despite the vast majority wanting
to. Women lose 18 percent of their earning power when they
take time out for childbearing and raising, and an alarming 37
percent of their earning power if they leave the workforce for
three or more years. A report in *Industrial and Labor Relations Review* found negative wage effects for mothers even *twenty years*
after they'd taken their time off.

Some women may simply feel these costs are too great to be borne, especially in uncertain economic times. Others may find workplace discrimination too dismaying to continue dealing with. Both real-world and laboratory experiments have repeatedly shown discrimination against mothers in the workplace, even in situations where women as a group were not discriminated against—even in situations in which childless women had an advantage over men. Mothers were perceived as both less committed to their careers and less competent. These factors, along with the structural lack of support for work-life balance, can help explain why 86 percent of highly qualified women who quit their jobs after having children cited workplace factors as the main reason why, according to a 2004 study in *The Annals of the American Academy of Political and Social Science*.

That's what they say for a while, anyway. Often the language of "choice" winds up being adopted by individual mothers, because to do otherwise is to paint yourself as a victim. Amy Cuddy of Northwestern's Kellogg School of Management pointed out that "People who've left promising careers to stay home with their kids aren't going to say, 'I was forced out. I really want to be there.' It gives people a sense of control that they may not actually have."

Looking at the ideology of motherhood (as compared to the economic reality), sociologist Alan Wolfe discovered a deep divide on the question of working versus stay-at-home mothers— a divide not between people but within them. Nearly half his study population was deeply ambivalent: "Longing for a world that no longer exists but having no intention of giving up the one that does, they are torn between nostalgia and necessity." That ambivalence can add fuel to the firewall between the two groups of mothers. A choice that, deep down, you feel uncomfortable about is often the one you'll most vehemently defend, because you need to prove to *yourself*, not only to the other person, that your decision was the right one.

So if you're a mother, respect the choices of those who differ from you. As with different parenting styles, it may ultimately wind up that you feel most comfortable with those with whom you have the most in common. But recognize the difficulty we all have in deciding whether or not to have children, and how to raise them if we do. Don't rush to judge—or rush to assume that you have been judged.

For example, take this modern-day, cocktail-party conversational impasse, the all-American question "What do you do?"— and the ensuing awkward silence when a woman says that she stays at home with her children. Reasonably, a stay-at-home mom often interprets the ensuing silence as judgment: "Well, household drudge, you clearly have nothing of interest to say to me, so I'm going to go talk to someone who has a life now. Buh-bye." But I realized a while back that I too tend to be struck mute in that situation, even though I believe she's made a perfectly valid choice. So why was I so at a loss for a follow-up? Because motherhood is so very *intimate*, while your job is part of your public persona that makes polite and sympathetic follow-up questions to people with jobs both appropriate and easy to think of:

"I'M A SALESCLERK." *"You must be glad the holidays are over! Was it awful?"*

"I'M A DOCTOR." *"What do you find most rewarding about that?"*

"I'M A WRITER." *"What kinds of things do you write about?"*

"I'M A PASTRY CHEF." *"How did you get started in that career?"*

See, you can't ask those kinds of things of a "mom":

"Really? How did you get started in that career?"
"Two bottles of pinot noir and a Barry White CD."

You can ask a mother about her children, of course, but there are perils there, too. If you ask a stay-at-home mom about her prior career, it might come across as, "So what did you used to do, back when you were a person?" Curiously, some stay-at-home moms tend to get tetchy about that.

Stay-at-home moms should be aware that the awkward silence may not indicate disrespect but a desire to honor the privacy of your family life. Try following "I stay home with my kids," with a conversational bridge—"and right now we're working on preschool applications. It's ridiculous! Midvale School for the Gifted expects a four-year-old to have a résumé!" or "I've been thinking about trying to find a gym with a childcare facility. Do you happen to know one?" An anecdote, a joke, a statement about your nonparental interests, a change of topics to current events—any of these can help keep your conversation alive.

· 6 ·

Private Parts

HEALTH

Fat naked man on subway: "I'm not ashamed of my body."
Jerry: "Exactly. That's your problem. You should be."

—"The Subway," *Seinfeld*

The heartache and the thousand natural shocks that flesh is heir to give rise to a thousand and one etiquette dilemmas. We are biological creatures, yet a good part of civilization consists of concealing our biological nature. Most of us can identify with both the fat naked man on the subway, proudly being the human animal he is, and also with Jerry, urging him to cover up, already. How do we walk the line between body shame and indiscretion? *Seinfeld* aside—because no one really takes etiquette tips from Larry David sitcoms, thank God—if you are comfortable and straightforward about your body, chances are others will be, too. It's people who act as though illness and embarrassment are huge, insurmountable *deals* who make other people feel the most awkward.

Most of the advice in this chapter will be focused on health issues as they play out in the workplace or in social situations with acquaintances or strangers. Your spouse, and by extension the rest of your family, promised to love you in sickness and in health; your coworkers did not. Hence, health and disability issues are most likely to cause awkwardness with people with whom we aren't on intimate terms, to whom we want to present ourselves as competent, sophisticated, and self-sufficient— and who want to see us as such.

When I examine these moments of halting interaction, I do it largely through the lens of sociologist Erving Goffman's 1963 masterpiece, *Stigma: Notes on the Management of Spoiled Identity*. Goffman analyzed social interaction as a kind of theater—all the world truly was a stage for him—in which people are playing various social roles. A "stigma" is an attribute that threatens to undermine the role you are playing at a given time. For example, I once got a desperate plea for advice from an emergency-room doctor who looked very young and disliked it when patients mentioned that fact. When patients mentioned his apparent youth, I suspect it made him feel undermined as an Authoritative Doctor. It disrupted his performance—his work as a doctor. It's no insult to be told you look young per se—I doubt Dr. Doogie would have been upset had he been carded by a fine-looking bartender who then expressed amazement at finding out his real age.* Being told he looked young didn't undermine his identity as an attractive hipster-about-town. But then, the patients who were commenting on his youth weren't trying to undermine his "doctor" identity—they were trying to transcend their own identity as patients. By showing that they could make small talk, they were saying, "Don't just see me as a lump

---

* The early-'90s cultural reference thereby giving away my own age.

of wounded flesh! I'm a real person, observant and socially competent!"

Sickness and disability can function as a stigma, especially in the workplace; the image of the productive and impersonal worker doesn't mesh well with that of the vulnerable and limited body. But the stigmatization of illness and disability isn't the product of late-modern capitalism. Prejudice against and discomfort with the physically different is seen in all times and cultures, and even in different species—Jane Goodall observed chimpanzees assiduously avoiding contact with other chimpanzees who were partially paralyzed. It's likely that they saw the disabled chimps as a sort of threat. I once had to intervene when my beloved dog, Milo—you'll meet him up close, and passionately, in the next chapter—attacked a three-legged dog. Milo is no bully who figured he could beat up on a dog who couldn't run away—he only becomes aggressive out of fear. That three-legged dog, merely by being different, scared the hell out of him.

What's up with that? Many reasons have been put forth for why fear and dislike of disabled and sick folks is so universal. One of the more compelling explanations, especially in light of disability prejudice among animals, is that it is an evolutionary mechanism. We quickly notice and seek to avoid people who don't look "normal" because whatever they have might be catching. Cruel, but adaptive. This psychological mechanism is a fairly blunt instrument—whether Og's leg fell off from leprosy or got chomped off by a crocodile, Oonah is going to stay away from him if she can, so that it doesn't happen to her.

Until they've had a while to get used to it, people are anxious in the presence of others who have diseases or disabilities, especially if the disease or disability is visible. Scholars have identified several factors that are likely to ratchet up discomfort with or prejudice against the sick or disabled:

- Threat: people whose diseases are contagious, or believed to be so, tend to have a harder time of it than noncontagious sick people.
- Controllability: if there's a cultural belief that you became sick or disabled through your own bad behavior, you're going to bear the brunt of more social prejudice.
- Disruptiveness: people whose bodily vulnerabilities require others to change their behavior create more anxiety in others.

(Together, the first two factors explain why HIV-positive people face far more prejudice than people with cancer.)

Treating the sick and disabled with the respect that they deserve requires something akin to a manual override of the monkey mind. Fortunately, we can do this. People who write about evolutionary psychology as though we are trapped in the Pleistocene, and like to use the word "hardwired" a lot, conveniently forget one fact: the main thing we humans evolved to do is to *learn* and *adapt*. That's our major strength as a species: we evolved the capacity to overcome our evolutionary heritage! There's a party trick for you.

And that's enough heavy theory for the moment. Let's talk about farting and pooping.

Gases, Liquids, Solids

Even the able-bodied and most flu-resistant among us will, occasionally, be betrayed by our own digestive system. As a general rule, civilized folk will protect others from any sounds or smells that may be displeasing, but even the greatest vigilance is sometimes not enough. Should you find your own barricades breached, a quick "excuse me" is sufficient.

This is the case for sounds; for smells, if there are several people in the room, you want to pretend it didn't happen. That's not the orthodox advice, but it's what everyone does, and what everyone, deep down, wants everyone else to do. Having once smelt it, no one is much comforted by knowing who dealt it. If you find yourself dealing them on a frequent basis, however, *see a doctor*. No one should have to dwell in a cube farm that smells like an actual *farm*. There might be a medical or nutritional solution for your problem. If there isn't, step outside when you need to, and don't be afraid to use air freshener.

The office bathroom can at times provide occasions for self-consciousness. Bathrooms are bathrooms, and there's nothing wrong with using them for the intended purposes. You can also, quite properly, groom yourself, brush your teeth, and floss in the office bathroom. What you cannot do is hold an impromptu sales meeting or take calls on your cell phone. If you're not supposed to pass gas in the conference room, then you shouldn't confer in the bathroom, either.

How to Be a Polite Sick Person, Minor Version

Advice givers are fond of decrying the practice of going to work when you're sick, criticizing the dysfunctionally macho work ethic that leads to this behavior and pointing out the illogic of attempting to boost productivity by coming in and getting everyone else all germy. They're right—but nothing's going to change. Sometimes you have to go to work when you're contagious. We don't treat the common cold as though it were smallpox. And many noncontagious maladies, like hay fever or a broken arm, still make work and social situations awkward.

- **Take visible precautions.** When you've got a cold, take every precaution to avoid passing it on, and take these precautions somewhat ostentatiously, so that people know you're looking out for them. Put on a little "security theater": you want not only to spare people from getting your cold, you want to spare them the *worry* that they are going to get your cold. So wash your hands longer and more thoroughly in the bathroom than you normally do. Don't leave used tissues on your desk, even if you used them only to wipe up a bit of spilled tea. Carry a small bottle of Purell with you and disinfect shared office equipment after handling it. Spray your phone with Lysol and keep the can out where others can see it. Don't partake of shared food or ask to borrow anyone's stapler. Toll a bell before you as you approach the cubicles of the untainted and scatter ashes on your head. (Well, perhaps not that.) And don't ever feel embarrassed saying, "I have a cold, so I can't shake hands" when introduced to someone. This is a courtesy that people truly appreciate. The warmest, most sincere hug in the world doesn't convey quite as much care and consideration for others as refusing to touch them when you're germy.

- **Apologize in advance.** If your cold is noisy—or if you have hay fever—send around an e-mail to your colleagues letting them know that you appreciate their patience until the hacking and schnortling subsides. People are generally willing to be awfully patient and good-natured as long as they feel they're being *recognized* for being patient and good-natured, and that whoever is inconveniencing them knows that they are being inconvenienced.*

- **Provide a *bit* of information—as much as you feel is necessary and comfortable.** Even when your illness or injury doesn't affect others, it's still a good idea to let people know what's going on if you are visibly or audibly sick or injured. You don't have to give everyone the full rundown of every highlight of the camping trip that left you with that nasty case of poison ivy, and exactly how much of your body it's covering, and what exactly you were doing with that cute wilderness guide that led you to get it *there*. A simple, "Do I look disgusting or what? At least the next time I go on an excursion in the wilds, I'll know how to identify poison ivy!" sufficiently acknowledges the scabby, oozing elephant in the room and makes others feel more comfortable.

It's not as though coworkers or other PTA members aren't noticing your rash or cast, even if they're too polite to say anything. Take control of your own information and set yourself, and everyone else, at ease. (This benefits you, too. People are staring when you're not looking and gossiping when you're not listening, but they'll do so less if you acknowledge whatever's wrong.) This is especially important for women who are injured in such a way that it looks as though they might have been the victims of domestic violence. It can be very upsetting for coworkers or

---

* Perhaps someday the airlines will figure this out, but I'm not holding my breath.

casual acquaintances to fear for your safety and well-being and not know if they should stage some sort of intervention.

How to Be a Polite Sick Person, Major Version

Sometimes you might just wish you did have poison ivy, because what you have is so much harder to live with and to explain to others. Disabilities, visible and invisible. The major kinds of illnesses—multiple sclerosis, cancer, HIV. Unfair though it might be, if you are living with a major medical condition, it is your responsibility to help other people cope with it. It is your right, too. Sick and disabled people develop a keen sense for what they can control in life and what they can't. One of the things that can be controlled is how you talk about your condition, what you ask of others, and how much you decide to hide or reveal—so take charge. In general, people will want to know two things about you: what's wrong with you and what they are supposed to do about it.

Explaining what's wrong with you

If you have a serious medical condition, whether chronic or acute, there are a lot of ways you can communicate about it. Many disease and disability foundations have business cards that give a few facts about the condition and a Web address that people can go to for more information. If you can't get these, you could always make up some cards like this for yourself—or ask a friend who is good at design and writing to do it for you. The card should say what your condition is, what you can and can't do because of it, refute any commonly held preconceptions, and tell people where on the Web to look for more information. (That seems like a lot to ask of a business-card-sized document, but you'd be surprised how much you can get across by using simple, direct language and a ten-point font.) Quickly letting people know what the deal is and where, if they desire, they can learn more will help take their minds off it, so they can start thinking about you as Latoya the marketing guru or Bob the bake-sale coordinator again.

If your condition is chronic but won't last forever—a battle with cancer, say—you might want to think about setting up a blog so that friends and family, especially those out of town, can keep up with the course of your treatment without having to hound you with questions. Again, if you're not that tech-savvy, recruit a friend who is. It's not that hard to set up a blog nowadays, and it's the kind of favor someone would be delighted to be asked to do. There are also specialized Web sites that prepackage a lot of the logistics, including guestbook and photo gallery pages, for you—caringbridge.com and carepages.com, to name two.

Blogs are a great way of keeping lots of people informed at once about the state of your mind and body, and if you don't necessarily want everyone in the world to be able to find it, you can set the security so that only people approved by you can get in.* Tell folks that the blog is "required reading" before talking to you about your illness. One thing to keep in mind, though— if your regular posting schedule falls off, people are going to worry like mad. So don't get in the habit of posting frequently. Set the expectation that you'll only post when you have news, or once a week, or some such. And if you have a bad enough time of it that you can't post yourself, ask someone else to step

---

* Temporary project blogs are a good way to keep friends up to date on all kinds of life projects, including happier ones such as adopting a child or taking a trip.

in and write up the information that you want people to know.

There are other options for information control, too. You can use the grapevine if you don't want to cope with a lot of public attention—talk to a friend or two about your situation and let them carry the information to others. And, of course, there's nothing wrong with flat-out stonewalling people, especially in a work setting. "I don't like to talk about health issues at work. Can we please stick to business?" I think a more open approach is kinder and less likely to make you the subject of rumors. But it's your damn disease, you get to make the call on whether you're going to talk about it.

Explaining what others should do about it

If you have a disease or disability that requires other people to modify their behavior in some way, don't be shy. Give people the basics on disability etiquette and what you would appreciate help with and what you can do for yourself perfectly fine, thank you. The most important thing is to be specific—rather than saying "Please be considerate of my blindness," a person could request, "Please announce yourself when you come into my office, and say the name of anyone else who is with you." You might feel compelled to add, "Because I'm *blind* and I *can't see them,* duh!" but add it silently, in your head. People can be amazingly bad at thinking through the implications of things, and you've probably also missed the point in some rather spectacular ways in your life.

You don't have to let this etiquette session turn into grill-the-sick-dude. It's about other people's behavior, not yours. You should provide reasons for why people need to do what you want them to do, but you're not obligated to tell them your entire life story and how you feel about it in order to get them to put the coffeepot down where you can reach it from your wheelchair. If the questions start, redirect with an authoritative, "I'd rather not talk about that. What I'd rather discuss is . . ."

How to Be a Polite Well Person

"Some nights, it was difficult to boil water and make something even as easy as mac and cheese from a box. Having it made [for us] was such a help."

—"Cancer Club" member

So, today you're feeling fit as a well-tuned Stradivarius, and it's all those other folks who are germing and coughing up your workplace and taking forever boarding the subway. The main thing to remember is—that's *today*. Tomorrow could well be a different story. Prejudice of any kind is abhorrent, but prejudice against the sick or disabled is not only evil but stupid (what an awesome combination!) because you could well be discriminating against your future self. So have a little patience and treat others as you would like to be treated *when*—not if—it happens to you.

Acknowledging that "when" can be very, very hard. Prejudice against the sick or disabled is wrong but understandable: most people are terrified of pain, illness, disability, and death, and our profound lack of control over all of the above. We want to believe that it can't happen to us. One of the ways we do this is by subscribing to what social psychologists call "just world theory"—the belief that the world is just, that people get what they deserve. Just-world theory is comforting—it lets you believe that you won't get cancer because you don't smoke, that you won't get raped because you don't wear short skirts, that you won't go bankrupt because you work hard and save.

Comforting—and wrong, both factually and morally. It's natural to look at someone who has suffered misfortune and immediately try to figure out why the misfortune happened and why, therefore, it could never happen to *you*. But remind yourself, after your monkey mind does that little self-serving exercise, that random bad things happen to people. It'll make you kinder to others and also much kinder to yourself when the bad things eventually come.

Being mindful around minor ailments

The major rule of minor ailments is that no one is coughing, sniffling, or sneezing to annoy *you*. Their symptoms are far more irritating to *them*, and it is good to keep this in mind. Of course, those symptoms would also be irritating to you if you had them, so there's nothing wrong with taking precautions to ensure that you don't catch them. "I hate to ask, but is what you've got contagious? If so, let's not shake hands/share a pizza/lick each other's money, because I've got a major project coming up and can't afford to get sick right now." Yes, it seems odd that you'd have to give a reason why you don't want to get someone else's cold, but it still seems more polite if you do.

The reason doesn't even have to be a terribly good one. Psychologist Ellen Langer and two colleagues did a wonderful study in 1978 in which an experimenter asked people if they'd mind if the experimenter cut ahead of them in a line to use a copier. The experimenters gave one of three reasons for the request: 1) no reason at all; 2) a good reason, such as "I'm in a big rush"; and 3) what Langer dubbed a "placebic" reason, "I have to make copies." People were much more likely to comply if they were given a reason—even a reason that really isn't a *reason*. The moral is, never waste mental energy coming up with an excuse; as long as what you say has the external features of an excuse, it will work just as well.

Being mindful around major ailments

If the major ailment is the kind of thing someone will be living with for a long time, like diabetes, multiple sclerosis, or an autoimmune disorder, take your cue from them on how they want to deal with it.

For some folks, it's important to feel out of the closet, and they'll openly refer to their condition and symptoms and be willing to educate others. Treat them as you would someone who has made a life choice different from yours. Listen in a way that makes them feel comfortable as they're talking, and ask questions if you're interested and don't if you're not.

Others consider their illness or disability to be personal and don't wish to bring it into the workplace or casual social situations. Follow their cue as well. Ask questions when they relate specifically to situations you'll be dealing with—for example, asking a diabetic colleague, "I'm picking up doughnuts for the meeting tomorrow. Would you like me to get you a muffin or a bagel, or will you just have coffee?" If you don't have a need to know, then keep in mind that your sick or disabled coworker or neighbor is not on this earth to educate you. Pretty much every unpleasant condition has its own foundation or support society these days, so if you're curious, Google it instead of turning to him as your boundless font of information. Don't pretend that you know more about his condition than he does; chances are he does indeed know about that new treatment or diet or genetic theory that's been all over the news, so shut up. Blogs can also serve as a great resource for learning how the other half lives; it's like eavesdropping, except people *want* you to do it! How cool is that? So if you're curious about what life is like for your coworker with MS, lurk on MS blogs for a while. I have found blogs to be an invaluable source of information on the thoughts and lives of people different from myself—from Mormons to stay-at-home moms to people with disabilities.

Being mindful around hospitalized folks

When people are seriously downed by something that's going to go away relatively soon—pneumonia, appendicitis, surgery, a bad accident—send them cards and goodies. Candy is nice for hospitalized people; if they can't eat it themselves, they can give it to the nurses. So, too, are sudoku or crossword books, magazines, DVDs, and other entertainment options appropriate to their interests and current level of cognitive functioning and physical coordination. Flowers are nice for people who like flowers but can be depressing for those who don't, or who are going to be in the hospital long enough that their bouquet will die and thus present a morose reminder of just how long they've been laid up. Plants may brighten up a hospital room but then will need to be taken home and cared for, so if the person didn't like plants before she was hospitalized, you can safely assume that her feelings didn't change because she broke her hip.

Cards and letters are good because they are unintrusive, and the stricken person can read them at leisure, in the moment when they feel good and energetic. Phone calls and visits are also welcome, but just as a patient may be bored and longing for company, he may also be sleep-deprived, grubby-feeling, and in need of privacy. So call first, and keep your calls short and your antennae up for how he really feels. The clever hospitalized person will appoint a relative or friend as a spokesperson, so that you can call or e-mail someone else to find out if visits are welcome and when, if crosswords are preferred to sudoku or flowers to candy, what the current prognosis is, and what sort of practical help the person needs now or when he returns home.

Helping effectively

"Let me know if you need anything." Are there seven more useless, impotent words in the English language? We all know the feeling of helplessness that descends upon us when we say this to someone who is sick or bereaved or otherwise having a time of it. Yet most of the time, we truly don't know what it is that would be helpful, because we don't live in close enough proximity to one another. I could support Mr. Improbable through a serious illness without asking him what, specifically, he wanted me to do, but that's only because I have years of experience supporting him through everyday life.

Of course, sick, bereaved, or otherwise distraught people, even if they take the offer seriously, don't have the emotional or intellectual energy to think up what would be helpful. That's what sickness and sadness do to you. And since you've made the offer—painfully inadequate though it be—the sick person feels the burden of thanking you for your good wishes, and somehow it's all back on her head again, which was never your intention.

So it's better to make some specific offers, tailored to what you really know you can deliver based on your own schedule and abilities. A few ideas:

- "I can give you two hours a week to clean your house, or help you pay bills or get through paperwork, or run errands."
- "I can take your kids/dog to the park on Saturday afternoons until your leg heals."

- "I can provide dinner once a week and organize other neighbors to provide it the other nights for the next month."
- "I can pick up your groceries every Tuesday when I make my grocery run."
- "I can help you write thank-yous to the people who sent flowers when your father died." (This, incidentally, is the only situation in which it is okay for a third party to take on someone's thank-you-note-writing chores, and it's a good thing to do.)
- "I can drive you to chemo."

The Web site lotsahelpinghands.com can also be useful in these cases. The site provides a group calendar that will allow friends, family, and neighbors to find out what needs to be done and who's doing it and when. You can also use the site to post updates.

The c-word

Cancer patients live in an in-between stage, because their illness—and the horrendous treatment—goes on so much longer than most illnesses do, yet isn't in the chronic category of, say, diabetes. In 2007, cancer survivor Darcy Davidson posted a brilliant rant on Craigslist*—which told everyone what *not* to say to people with cancer including:

- **Don't share sympathetic tales of "death by cancer."** "For some reason, it occurred several times that when I told someone what I was going through (which is kinda awkward anyway)," Darcy wrote, "they would say something to the effect of *"Ohhhh,* my [mother, sister,

---

*Her bilingual blog is at http://conlimonsal.blogspot.com.

aunt, grandmother, insert any other relative or even remote acquaintance here] just died last year of cancer" or "Right, my [insert distant relative here] died of Hodgkin's." When people are fighting a long-term illness, they don't want to hear that.

• **Don't make chemotherapy small talk.** "Comments like 'How's your hair doing?,' 'Wow, it's really thinning out!,' 'So is your hair just coming out in handfuls?,'" and 'Is that a wig?' are not helpful," she wrote, "and *will* make me cry. If you think this is stupid or oversensitive, let me say it again: next time you get cancer let me know how this goes."

• **Don't promise more than you can deliver.** "In the beginning everyone called all the time, offered to go to chemo with me, sent lots of e-mails, came over to visit when I was sick . . . but after the months drag on it's like people get sick of it," she reported. "I understand that 'cause I got pretty sick of it too. I got sick of calling in to work, not doing anything fun, not seeing anyone . . . even just answering the damned 'How are you feeling?' question. . . . I felt like it was better to lie and say 'fine' than to say how I really felt because people kind of don't know how to react or don't want to hear it."

As good as that advice is, Darcy didn't say what you *ought* to say or do when a friend, relative, or coworker is diagnosed.

So I requested that survivors share with me with their advice for people who want to support a friend, coworker, or neighbor who has cancer. I can't do any better than they did.

✦ The best verbal support is the kind that doesn't make me have to explain how I feel. Don't ask questions. Make a pleasant statement, like, "It's good to see you!" Or, "I've been thinking of you."

I don't want to burden someone with a request. So call and say, "Hey, I'm headed to the market, is there anything you need that I can get while I'm there?" or "We're going apple picking (or whatever) and I know you bake a great apple pie. Can I bring you a bag of apples?"

I'm on the prayer list at church and I get several cards a week from members of the congregation. If you know someone who is having an extended tough time, no matter the reason, pick up a few cards, write a note in each, and address them. Then mail one per week. Those constant snail-mail smiles are a wonderful warm hug.

✦ What helped the most, besides taking a more active role in my treatment, were those who found it in themselves to keep some kind of "normalness" in my life. There were many things I could not do, but we found ways to do things that never—not once—reminded anyone, especially myself, that I was sick.

Sometimes it was as simple as having an entire girls' night out where not one of us acknowledged my having to occasionally disappear to the ladies' room to upchuck those garlic fries I knew I should never have eaten in the first place; where no one would mention that my bandanna was slipping. No words, no looks, never a break in the conversation—just a quick, surreptitious, gentle nudge to put it back into place.

For me, the best thing some of my friends were able to do was to find ways to treat me as a person—not a person with cancer. Each one of us is unique, just as our particular diagnoses and prognoses are. No one thing will work for everyone. But if you are lucky enough to have friends who know you well—really well—they will know those little things that should not change—cannot change—just because you have this disease. I guess—no, I know—I am very lucky.

Yes, you can take a break to go wipe your eyes and blow your nose before we finish up the chapter. I certainly had to.

Being mindful around people with disabilities

There's a whole field known as "disability etiquette." If you're working with a person with a disability, you should look into the specific issues for that person's group, since I cannot provide a comprehensive guide in the space of these pages. Here, however, are the basics:

- **It's "person with a disability," not "disabled person."** This isn't a bit of politically correct hairsplitting; it reflects a serious philosophical difference.* "Person with a disability" means person *first*. Disability *second*. "Person with a disability" means that the disability does not define the person's life or humanity. It is probably not the most important thing in her world and may not occupy a major role in her life story. Her cane, hearing aid, wheelchair, or oxygen tank aren't encumbrances but devices of liberation:

---

* Many things dismissed as politically correct hairsplitting do, in fact, reflect serious differences, so the next time you encounter some, spend a bit of time thinking through what's behind it. Doing so will make you a kinder and more intelligent person.

wings, not shackles. So, person with a disability, "wheelchair user" not "wheelchair bound," and so forth.

This can be hard for the temporarily abled to understand—but think about yourself and your own "disabilities." Do you wear corrective lenses? Do you need a step stool to get items off the top shelf of the grocery store or library? Did your concert-going years leave you with minor hearing loss? Do you have aches and pains? Most people are "disabled" in some way or another. Disability is not a black-or-white concept—it's a continuum. I have a friend with perfect pitch; do I consider myself "disabled" next to him? Are those of us with insensitive palates "disabled" in comparison to those supertasters we read about in chapter 1? Most of us would like to have abilities beyond those that we do, hence the popularity of superheroes; very, very few of us consider our lives not worth living.

It's easy to overestimate the impact of a disability on a person's life, because when you're thinking about the disability, you're not thinking about everything else the person has going on. Nobel laureate Daniel Kahneman identifies this as the "focusing illusion"—whenever we consider the impact of a single factor on quality of life, we overestimate it. We think it would be much, much nicer to be rich than it actually is, because we're thinking only about the lovely money and not thinking about the fact that we'd still have many of the same problems *with* it that we do *without* it. We think it would be much, much worse to have a disability than it actually is, because we focus on all the prohibitions and inconveniences the disability would introduce into our lives, and forget that there would still be love, work, chocolate, mystery novels, and music to enjoy.

People with disabilities—minor or major—tend not to obsess over what they can't do; they energetically tackle that which they can, instead, just like the rest of us.

- **Take people with disabilities at their word for what they can or can't do.** Don't make assumptions about their capabilities; ask. And believe them: If they say they can do something, don't assume they're cowboying up in order to appear "normal"; they know their bodies' limits and capacities as well as you know your own. (Better, probably.) If they say they can't do something, believe them. It doesn't matter if you can't see a disability—not everyone who looks healthy is. It doesn't matter if it's a disease you don't "believe" in. Your beliefs about fibromyalgia aren't relevant. Your beliefs about a person's absolute right to make decisions about things that affect her body are. Likewise, if you offer help, don't be offended if your offer is rejected. Trust people to know what help they need and what help they don't, and remember that your offer was meant to be about *their* needs, not *yours*. It's not the job of people with disabilities to make you feel all warm and glowy inside like a character in an After School Special.

- **If a person has equipment, such as a wheelchair or cane, don't touch it.** It's part of his body, and grabbing the equipment is as big a faux pas as tugging on Superman's cape, pulling the mask off the Lone Ranger, or messing around with Jim. If a person with a disability is with another person, address questions meant *for* the person with a disability *to* her, not to the other person as though she wasn't there or isn't capable of speaking for herself.

• **Pay attention to the context.** Think things through. Don't yell "Look out!" to a blind person, because they won't know what to do. They *can't* look out; they're *blind*. Be specific: Yell "Angry pit bull at five o'clock" or "The door's closed" or "Stop! There's a banana peel in front of you." Don't turn your face away from a hard-of-hearing person who is relying to some extent on your lip movements. On the other hand, don't freak out if you make this kind of mistake; until accommodating the person's needs becomes second nature to you, mistakes are inevitable. No one expects you to be psychic, only to be paying attention.

• **Talk to them.** The research about people with disabilities in the workplace that I find saddest are the studies that show how little ordinary conversation they have with their colleagues. Their nondisabled coworkers are often uncomfortable with them and talk only about the disability itself or about purely task-focused matters. Imagine workplace life without gossip and banter! Now there's something that would really bring a person down. People with disabilities have hobbies, favorite television shows, opinions on fashion and sports, holiday plans, and irritating family members, the same as everyone else does. So hit them up with some small talk.

One thing you don't need to worry about is using bodily metaphors around people with disabilities. There's nothing wrong with saying, "See you later!" or even "Do you see what I mean?" to a blind person, or "Let's get this project off to a running start" to someone in a wheelchair. People with disabilities understand the concept of figures of speech as well as anyone else, and they dislike awkward silences and long rambling apologies delivered in an agony of self-consciousness as much as anyone else, too. You do want to avoid using disability-negative metaphors like "Relationships are a blind spot for me" or "High school gym class crippled my self-esteem." And don't use "retarded" or "retard" as an insult, which is a rather junior-high level of discourse, anyway. It's far more dignified to accuse someone of having cooties.

People with disabilities generally don't expect kids to be supercool about it. Some probably do, but these are the kinds of people who think children should not be allowed in public until they have mastered the protocol skills of a senior ambassador to a strategically important country, and such people, whether disabled or not, are clearly out of touch with reality. (The fact that people with disabilities are people means that statistically a certain percentage of them are going to be jerks.) So if your kid does the point-and-stare, grab her, say, "That's rude," apologize to the stared-at person, and move on. If your kid asks a rude question, explain, "We don't ask people we don't know questions about their bodies," apologize, and move on. The questioned person might choose to answer the child's question or not. You should answer your children's questions as soon as you get home; look stuff up with them together, if you need to. (Encourage their curiosity enough and who knows? Someday you might get to say, "My son/daughter, the doctor!") Let your children know that there isn't anything to be ashamed of about the human body, ever, but that at the same time, people have the right to privacy, and *this* is why we don't comment on others' bodies in public.

Fat Hate

"The preoccupation with fat has become a struggle between good and evil, between the baseness of human instinct and the glory of rational restraint. In low-fat theology, dietary prudence equals virtue; a taste for fat is immoral."
—Molly O'Neill, food columnist

Fat people, like everyone else, may or may not be sick or disabled. I am including them in this chapter because they are almost universally treated as though they are one or both and as though it's entirely their fault, too.

I've always been aware that fat people are the victims of prejudice, but until I started writing the "Miss Conduct" column I didn't understand the extent of it. Then I discovered that whenever I suggest treating fat people with courtesy, I would receive not only letters disagreeing with me but actual *hate mail*.* People really, truly believe that it is not only acceptable but morally right—a sort of duty—to treat fat people with disdain.

I'm sad to say that I've been inculcated with enough societal garbage that I occasionally hate my own body—but as a thin (white, able-bodied, etc.) person, I cannot fathom what it must be like to have others take it upon themselves to hate my body *for* me. If you think fat people have no self-control, pause a moment to think of the remarkable restraint they exercise given the cruelty and prejudice they face every day.

Fat people are seen as lazy, lower-class, unintelligent, dirtier, and emotionally incontinent. Fat people, including adolescents,

---

* The other two groups of whom this is true are smokers and Muslims. I'm determined that whenever I encounter fat, smoking Muslims, I shall wrap them in huge weepy hugs while proclaiming my svelte, allergy-ridden Jewish love—and probably succeed in scaring the hell out of a good plurality of them.

are more likely to suffer from depression, to think about and attempt suicide, and to be socially isolated. They are less likely to be hired for jobs and less likely to receive financial support for college *from their own families*. Fat prejudice begins as early as toddlerhood, and schoolchildren rank fat children as less socially desirable than children with crutches, wheelchairs, amputated limbs, and facial disfigurement.

There's an increasing amount of research suggesting that weight might not be under a person's control, and that the dangers of obesity may be overstated. There's an *overwhelming* amount of research showing that diets don't work. But from the point of view of courtesy, it's irrelevant whether fat people can "help it." Tanning is clearly bad for your health and entirely a matter of choice, but we don't mock and shame the tanned, or yell, "Hey, leatherface!" at them from a car window. And fat prejudice hurts everyone, including the thin. For years I had horrendous exercise and diet habits, but because my body naturally settles into a slender-but-sturdy range, doctors assumed I was doing everything right. I wasn't, and some very real health problems were being neglected.

Fat people know that they are fat and are aware that they take up more room than thin people, so if you feel you need to recommend a sturdier chair or want to suggest a different table at the restaurant, you're not going to surprise them. Be straightforward—and unembarrassed. Don't argue with a fat person when they mention that they are fat. The message sent by "I don't think of you as fat" is much the same as "I don't think of you as black," and it's not a flattering message. It's the message that "I think most people like you are sort of stupid or disgusting, but you're not like them; you're one of the good ones." Charming!

Conversely, though, if you are fat, cut some slack to a person who offers the "I don't think of you that way" pseudo-nicety. No, it's not a nice thing to hear, but he might not yet realize how it sounds. I've said it myself, before I really thought it through, because to me "fat" means "spherical," and if a woman has an hourglass figure, no matter how many hours are in it, I don't think of her as fat but as *voluptuous*. If someone clearly does mean "Oh, you're not like those disgusting fat people," however, you have my blessing to respond to "I don't think of you as fat" with "Well, I don't think of you as thin."

If you are not fat, don't try to create a bond by discussing your own struggles to lose five pounds. If that's all the weight you need to lose to fit societal norms, you're not living in the same world as a fat person is. You're behaving *exactly the same* as a bad rich friend who complains to a poor friend about all the capital gains taxes she had to pay this year.

Even if I can't convince you of the wrongness of fat prejudice, look at it this way: why contribute to a self-fulfilling prophecy? Say you hate fat people because you think they're lazy and stupid. Treating someone as if they are lazy and stupid will in many cases lead to them acting that way around you. You've just increased your likelihood of being annoyed by fat folks.

So I entreat you: don't discriminate against fat people, and don't make assumptions about their morality, love life, athleticism, intelligence, or passion for life. Or anyone's, really, based on their physical condition. Eat your veggies and exercise as you will, bad luck and genetics can get us all in the end. It's the tragedy of our animal nature.

For the comedy-of-errors of our animal nature, continue to the next chapter.

· 7 ·

The Best Friend

PETS (AND OTHER PASSIONS)

"If you get to thinking you're a person of some
influence, try ordering somebody else's dog around."
—Will Rogers

Ah, dogs. As a social lubricant they are second only to
alcohol. As a social irritant, they are second only to alcohol. And like booze, dogs have been part of human society
almost since we *became* human. And as the most social of pets,
they are the ones that most often bring their owners into contact with people. Strangers aren't likely to pet your Jack
Dempsey fighting fish without permission, and if a ferret sticks
its nose in your crotch you are probably in a Farrelly Brothers
movie, which puts you well beyond the reach of etiquette advice. So while the recommendations for handling pets apply to
all animals—and other enthusiasms—I'll let the family dog drag
us around the block of pet psychology and etiquette.

The research is mixed on the extent to which having pets im-
proves physical health, but there are some intriguing studies that
show that having pets is good for social health—and not just the
owner's, either. Pet ownership provides what economists call

"positive externalities" and everyone else calls "nice side effects."
Researchers on human-animal interaction have found that people
with pets get out more and tend to perceive their neighborhoods
as friendlier places than people who don't have pets do. Happily,
even people without pets felt that having people walking dogs on
the street made their neighborhood seem safer, and that having
dog-walking neighbors helped them to get to know and recognize
the people who lived around them.

Certainly my own experience bears this out—in the first year
that we had Milo, Mr. Improbable and I spoke to more people in
our neighborhood than we had in all the years before we got him.
In a time when social critics decry the increasing isolation of
modern life—with its lack of neighborhood associations, block
parties, and bowling leagues—the kind of camaraderie a dog can
bring into your life is precious. Among dog lovers, there is a kind
of easygoing favor doing and freemasonry that can be difficult to
come by today.

The ability of dogs to bring people in closer contact with one
another was illustrated movingly in a post-9/11 essay published
in the online magazine *Slate* by Ahmed Tharwat, a Muslim immigrant from Egypt. Dogs are unclean in the Islamic tradition;
they're not forbidden, but it can be a great nuisance for an observant Muslim to try to keep a dog while maintaining laws
about ritual cleanliness. Finally cajoled into getting a beagle
puppy by his daughter, Tharwat then discovered that:

> People on the street, in their cars, in the parking lot, and at
> the supermarket were giving me a new look—a friendly
> one. Strangers who used to skillfully avoid eye contact
> now wanted to engage me in warm conversation. . . . As a
> hyphenated-American, I discovered that owning a dog eas-
> ily accomplished what many diversity training programs

have failed to do for years. Regardless of our race, color, religion, or country of origin, we were one community of civilized dog lovers.

He ended his essay by urging Arab-Americans to "get a puppy, now that you need a real friend."

Yet, for all their ability to bring us together, pets can also be another fault line in modern life. The evolutionary history of dogs (and to a lesser extent other domesticated animals), and research on the psychology of cuteness and disgust, helps explain why people have such strong feelings, positive and negative, about pets.

Paw de Deux (a/k/a "Dancing with Wolves")

"What would the first dogs have been like? . . . Craven scavengers slinking around in filth and waste, disease-ridden lowlifes scratching at fleas and mange."

—Jake Page

Lovely image, isn't it? How did we wind up sharing our lives with dogs, anyway? The favored just-so story for some time was a vaguely romantic notion of a little cave kid enchanted by a wolf cub, and his wise, kindly cave dad realizing that the cub, trained and grown, could help out with hunting and guarding the cave. But increasing evidence—from archaeology, DNA, animal ethology, and the way humans and feral dogs relate in contemporary cultures—has pretty well put paid to that charming tale.

What appears to have happened, instead, is that dogs chose *us*—or, rather, our garbage dumps. The earliest dogs were scavengers, living near but not in human settlements and eating refuse.* After generations and generations of living in proximity in this fashion, the evidence suggests, we humans at some point decided that if the dogs weren't going away, we might as well invite them in and let them keep us warm at night. And the dogs said, "Yes!" and wished they had opposable thumbs so they could pump their little fists. Their plan had worked, and our destinies were now entwined in a strange pas de deux of love and disgust.

Love

We'll start with love. Why do we love our dogs? Mostly, because they are an unparalleled example of survival of the cutest. In order to get close enough to people to scavenge effectively, protodogs developed a raft of behaviors and postures to convey their harmlessness and submission: the slink; the cower; the worshipful glance. Prehistoric life being what it was, I'm guessing the occasional ego boost from a dog might have felt pretty good. Dogs that couldn't deliver the message of "I'm completely harmless and live only to lick the crumbs from your not-yet-invented table" were more likely to be seen as a threat and driven off or killed.

After full domestication, the rewards for being appealing became even greater. The best-looking, most trainable, most charming dogs were the ones most likely to be given food and protected. They got pretty good at figuring us out, too. Dogs outperform much smarter animals than themselves in tests of social cognition. In one experiment by Brian Hare, for example, animals were brought into a room with two boxes, one of which held

---

* Stop to think for a minute about what humans would have deemed unfit for consumption back in the Pleistocene epoch. No wonder dogs will eat anything.

food. A person would indicate (by looking, touching, or pointing) which box it was. Wolves don't take the hint. *Chimpanzees* don't take the hint. But dogs do—even puppies that have had minimal contact with humans. They're born with it.

So on the dog side, you have a species that has been selected, over millennia, for optimal appeal. On the human side, you have a species with an innate need to be near and care for small cute things—and also an innate tendency to project human emotions onto practically everything that moves. (A lot of this goes back to the "intention detection" we discussed in the religion chapter.) We look into the big pleading eyes and see reverent admiration there. We hear the contented sigh as the dog settles in for the night and hear trust and faith there. We touch the warm luxurious fur and feel love there.

Disgust

We are also disgusted by dogs. Owned dogs are loved, but feral dogs are considered unclean, repellent vermin, and for rather good reason. "Dog" is an insult in just about every language.

Disgust is one of six "basic" emotions, which means emotions that are shared across all cultures.* The purpose of disgust, it seems, is to keep us away from things that can make us sick. The more something looks like a disease threat, the more disgusting it is—towels stained with blue or green dye aren't judged as disgusting, but towels stained with dye that looks like pus or excrement are. Cultures vary to some extent in

---

* The others, identified by psychologist Paul Ekman and his colleagues, are anger, sadness, surprise, fear, and happiness. Disgust is so basic that humans, across all cultures, make the same facial expression, marked by raised upper lips, wrinkled noses, and flared nostrils. Try making the face: We can smell disgust, and our faces are trying to get rid of it.

what they consider disgusting, especially around food, but the gross-out factor is universal for things like rotten meat and decomposing vegetable matter, blood, excrement, and dead bodies. It's worth noting that this list pretty much spells "party supplies" to your average dog.

We're not born with the capacity to feel disgust, a truth that most parents can illustrate with a repertoire of hilarious yet disturbing stories. We have to learn what to be grossed out by. This is why, often, little kids will get it "wrong"—not only will they fail to be disgusted by something that should disgust them, but they will do things like hold a crumpled, but clean, paper tissue at arm's length and make a thoroughly skeeved expression. They haven't yet figured out that crumpled Kleenex are only disgusting if they're used.

Disgust works beautifully to keep us away from pathogens. As useful as that is evolutionarily, though, it would be a bad thing if we couldn't overcome it, because we would freak out and abandon our babies in the forest the first time they made doody. So love can conquer disgust. One delightful experiment had mothers smell-testing their own babies', and other babies', dirty diapers in a blind test. The title sums up the results: "My Baby Doesn't Smell as Bad as Yours: The Plasticity of Disgust." As the authors put it, "We reasoned that a mother's care for her infant is inextricably linked to frequently encountered disgust elicitors (e.g., vomit, urine, and feces) and that disgust to such elicitors represents an obstacle to care."

So while dogs can be objectively disgusting, when it's your dog (or cat, ferret, or fighting fish), you don't even notice. Which can be problematic, because other people *do*, and we want our pets to enhance our social lives, not detract from them.

Getting Positive Externalities from Your Dog

Question: *I just hosted an open house for friends at my new home. I added "no pets, please" to the invitation, as my husband is allergic to dogs and cats. One of my girlfriends, who takes her dog everywhere, was angered by my request. How can I make her understand that I was right to tell my friends not to bring their pets?*

You have to love those "Ten Tips to Improve Your Health" articles that tell you, "Science has shown that having pets benefits your health. So get a cat!" It's not like getting enough exercise or eating your veggies; if you really hate cats, getting one is not going to improve your health or overall life. Before you and your pet can be good for other people, you have to be good for each other. Only get a pet if you really want one and are ready to make the commitment to it. If you like dogs but don't have the time, space, or money for one, borrow a neighbor's dog for the occasional walk.

Because walking is really the key. Dogs are not going to do anything for you socially if all you do is let them out in the backyard a couple of times a day. Walk your dog, and use the walks as opportunities to get to know your neighbors as much as possible. Australian researchers looking into the social benefits of pet owning point out that pet owners often create informal favor networks—initially based around petsitting but often spreading into other domains as well. This kind of thing is healthy for a community, so try to get a vigorous social exchange going. And make sure that non–pet owners are included in the group, too.

Manners for dogs

Your dog can't improve your social life if it has no social skills of its own. The first commandment for a dog owner is Thou Shalt Train Thy Dog. Training means learning how your dog sees the world and disciplining yourself enough to communicate with your dog consistently. In short, training a dog is about training yourself. A trained dog is a happy dog and a dog that people will enjoy being around. Sometimes people think they're trammeling a dog's free nature by training it, which is nonsense. Dogs are social pack animals, and they have a better sense of natural etiquette than we do. You just have to let them know what's expected.

This can be difficult, because a dog's brain works very differently from yours. So get a trainer who knows what a dog thinks you're saying and what they're saying back to you. You want a trainer who is consistent and gentle, treats both you and your dog with respect, and exudes a sense of maturity and self-control. Do not go to a trainer who has his own ego invested in the process, who appears angry, spacey, or New Agey, or who insists on working with your dog in your absence. (In general, really, it's a good idea to avoid people who are ego-invested, angry, spacey, New Agey, or insist that you "trust me.")

A trainer or behaviorist should be able to teach you not only how to control your dog but how to read the signals your dog is sending out. Is your dog frightened? Angry? Does it really "just want to be friends" or is it asserting dominance? Learning how to interpret your dog's signals is essential for good manners and, more important, safety. Learn the signals that your dog uses when it's scared or nervous, and don't let people tease or bother your dog if it's showing those signs. You don't owe people access to your pets as a hosting responsibility, and if guests get insistent about that, shut things down fast.

Sooner or later, of course, your dog will screw up. Everyone's dog does. It will start a fight with another dog in the park, eat the houseguest's underwear, growl at the neighbor's new baby, "mark" your sister-in-law's new sofa.* This happens to all dog owners sooner or later. When it happens to you, you remove the dog, apologize, take whatever remedial action is necessary, apologize again, and get on with your life. And you do it all very calmly. Pet owners, like parents, often have their own self-image so wrapped up in the good behavior of their charges that they can overreact quite badly to an incident of misbehavior—by either over-apologizing or offering defensive excuses. If your dog (or, for that matter, your child) is behaving badly, don't get all frazzled and expect others to sympathize with you as though you were the victim. You're not the victim, you're the grown-up, and you need to cowboy up and act like one.

Diversity training is the new obedience training

Here is a sad fact about dogs: they can be extremely bigoted. Dogs notice the differences between people, and if a dog has a bad experience with, say, a cigar-smoking man of color in his fifties or sixties, then that dog may well dislike people of that description forever. This can be embarrassing for owners who want their dogs to appreciate the value of diversity. It can also cause them to question themselves, as there is a folk belief that dogs "pick up" their owners' prejudices. "You're sending your fear down the leash!" I have heard more than once. (Okay, it's

---

* Milo actually went one better than that one memorable day and peed on my sister-in-law herself. Thanks for being such a good sport about that, Jane.

Milo who hates tobacco-reeking men of color.) This is not the case. Dogs are entirely capable of generating prejudices of their own. I'm not the slightest bit frightened of sixty-year-old Latino cigar smokers. I'm frightened of entitled-acting fraternity jocks, whom Milo usually approaches with a big grin and hind wiggles. I have my issues, he has his. If your dog is a bigot, either minimize his exposure to the kinds of people your dog doesn't like or work through the issue, with a trainer or by yourself, if you know how.

Because of this, shall we say, "profiling" tendency among dogs, it is a good idea to expose them to as many different kinds of people (and dogs; they can develop breed biases as well) as you can when you get a puppy. If Milo had met lots of people of color, and smokers, before the Bad Thing happened, he probably wouldn't have developed the prejudice he has. But he was a suburban backyard dog before he came to us and didn't get to see much of the world, and like everyone who lives a sheltered and monotonous life, he got a little crusty and reactionary because of it.

You may also want to desensitize your pets to people with disabilities, if you have a good relationship with a friend or neighbor who has a disability and is willing to work with you. Even without a prior bad experience, animals sometimes strongly dislike people with disabilities. Movement is animals' language, and someone who doesn't move the way most people do can be scary, as we saw in chapter 6. Not all pets will have this fear, but better to desensitize your dog early than have it go after some sweet old grandpa with a walker. Even if your dog isn't an ableist bigot, keep the differing perspectives of children and the elderly in mind. A twenty-five-pound dog could yank a wee grandma off her feet without even trying if it spies a squirrel during a leisurely walk or if grandma tries to play tug-of-war with it. And two thirty-pound dogs wrestling can be quite amusing to adults but terrifying to a kindergartner who may not weigh that much more herself.

Don't come off like a people hater

Pets can improve your social life but only insofar as you're dealing with people who like, or at least are willing to tolerate, animals. Not everyone does, and there's not much you can or should do about it. Pet owners are not going to convert any animal haters by forcing them to interact with Max or Sheba against their will—and Max and Sheba, like all innocent animals, deserve ever and only to be in the company of those who appreciate them. Pets should always be crated or confined when guests who are not comfortable with them are coming over.

Don't assume that your pet is invited everywhere you are. Don't assume your pet even *wants* to be invited everywhere you are; animals don't like novelty and are peculiarly immune to the charms of weddings, gallery openings, and NASCAR rallies. And homes that aren't pet-proofed can be dangerous. Don't insist that other people consider your pet a member of your family—especially so if they're asthmatic. That's a formula for getting yourself removed from future invites and friendships.

If you're visiting someone who is friends with your pet as well as you, it's okay to ask if you can bring Max along. But don't ask every time unless you don't have to ask—that is, if your friends are also dog owners, and it's taken for granted that the dogs socialize when you do. If you've asked once or twice, and the next time your friends invite you over they don't add, "Oh, and bring Max, too," then take it as a hint that Max is not as welcome as you thought, and stop asking.

Then, of course, you don't want to come off like a crazy cat lady, or dog guy, or, ah, pet person. People who don't have pets often harbor a vague suspicion that pet owners like animals better than people and are a little touched in the head. Do what you can to dispel this stereotype when you're with non-animal lovers (you can let your enthusiasms run off leash with your other pet-owning friends). Do not, for example, compare your pets to children around people who have children, without some serious caveats. However attached you may be to your animals, they are not your children. They just aren't, and the depth and nature of love and pain that animals bring to our lives is qualitatively different. At least it should be—if you truly find yourself thinking of a pet as a baby, get therapy, for the animal's sake as well as your own. Making your pet into something it cannot be is cruel.

You can, without giving offense, note the comparisons that do exist between being a pet owner and a parent (which is different from comparing the pet itself to a child). Keep your observations light, rather than attempting deep psychological insight or tales of major joys and triumphs. A mother would have every right to be offended if I compared my struggles with teaching Milo to heel with her difficulties helping her dyslexic daughter learn to read. But I've had many a happy moment sharing tales of the difficulties new parents and owners have in simply keeping track of all the gear (leashes, poop bags, toys, diapers, towels) or the songs we make up to sing to our charges when we're puttering around the house.*

Curb conspicuous spending and extreme claims about your pet. Your cat is not psychic and your dog does not understand English. If you think otherwise, study up on animal behavior for

---

* A particular favorite in our household of *Monty Python* fans: "Oh he's a Milo dog and he's okay / He sleeps all night and he poops all day."

a bit and learn to appreciate your pet for its actual nature and abilities. I certainly agree that dogs and cats can *act* as though they are psychic or have a deep intuitive understanding of us. But these behaviors are the result of instinctive behaviors and sensory systems that go far beyond our own. You'll get more respect from non–animal lovers—and probably from your pet, as well—if you acknowledge your pet's limitations.

And while you have every right to spend a significant percentage of your disposable income on your pet, keep it to yourself if you do. Bragging that you spend an hour every night preparing Sheba's home-cooked dinner of organic grain-fed chicken livers is not going to make people think, "Wow, what a great cat owner." It will make them think you are nuts. And it will make them wonder if all cat owners don't succumb to insanity eventually. And then they will be less likely to adopt a cat themselves. And a shelter cat who needs a home will die. So remember: every time you brag about your pet, God kills a kitten.

Mitigate the disgust factor

As noted, love conquers disgust. Remember the famous "tampon" conversation between Prince Charles and Camilla Parker Bowles? When you acquire a pet or child (or highborn mistress, for all I know), your disgust parameters change so quickly you might not even realize it. So if you have a pet, it's important to keep in mind that while your disgust parameters have changed, those of the people around you have not. People who don't have dogs find it very disconcerting to converse with a neighbor who is casually swinging a poop bag around. And they don't want to hear you talk about your pet's—or your child's—poop, either. Why are parents and pet owners so obsessed with poop, the pet- and child-free ask? Because when you are responsible for the health and well-being of dependents who cannot speak, their daily dump is one of the key indicators you have about their health. Hence, it's interesting. To the parents and owners, that is. Not to anyone else.

Animal lovers rightly believe that pet hair is the only sort of fur one can wear with a clear conscience. Non–pet owners, however, feel that cat or dog hair is not the perfect complement to a well-chosen outfit. If your furry pets are allowed on furniture, provide lint rollers to guests and offer them towels to sit on. Also, keep bottles of hand sanitizer prominently displayed in every room. Knowing that a visit to your home doesn't invariably involve being covered in pet hair and germs will make non–animal lovers much more comfortable. Wash or disinfect your own hands conspicuously before preparing food or drinks, or touching a child; this, too, will ease your guests' concerns.

Getting Positive Externalities from Other People's Dogs

If you don't have a dog, you can still get the benefits that they bring to the neighborhood, if you're willing to learn a bit about them and put up with the occasional eccentricities of their owners. If you've got some trepidation about dogs, ask a friend who's knowledgeable about them to teach you how to read their body language and interact appropriately.* Dogs can be hard to read at first, and a person who didn't grow up with them—or who grew up with some badly trained or unsocialized ones—

---

* People generally adore being asked to share their expertise, and spending an afternoon having a friend teach you how to interact with dogs, knit, change the oil in your car, or make a soufflé is cheap and fun entertainment. Don't be shy about requesting life lessons!

has every reason to approach them with hesitation. A doggie smiling looks an awful lot like a doggie baring its teeth. The plastered-down ears that are the canine equivalent of a friendly, submissive "G'day, guvnor!" look an awful lot like the plastered-down ears that mean "I'm going to eat your face."

But while it's easy to develop a fear of dogs, becoming seriously phobic about them can be socially disabling. It's like being afraid of bicycles; they're everywhere. If you have phobias—about animals or anything, really—do everything you can to avoid passing your fears on to your children. As a safety measure, children should be taught how to approach dogs and how to tell when a dog is dangerous.

You can ask pet-owing friends to confine their animals when you come over, and this is a request that should always be honored. If a friend is unwilling to do so, I would seriously question that person's judgment, if not the entire relationship. If your host seems reluctant to lock up Toby during the dinner party, however, and you don't want to have a big discussion about it, you could always try making an argument from the standpoint of the pet's welfare: "I'm so nervous around dogs/cats and bad with them, and I know they're really sensitive to people's emotions, so I'm worried that they'll pick up on my feelings and get agitated themselves." Yes, you may feel like you're selling out the entire human race if you say this, but there's a good chance it will work. I'm only offering it as an option. When you're in public, however, you can't avoid dogs and their owners—and, of course, I'm arguing that you don't want to, because you can meet some great people that way.

*There are few positive externalities in a
small-claims court or emergency room*

Of course, before all those lovely relationships blossom, you have to make sure that nothing horrendous happens. The most important principle in human-animal interaction is safety, and safety is the responsibility of the owner. Don't be offended if someone removes his pet from you or tells you how to hold or touch it. You might be alarming the animal without realizing it. Do not continue doing something to a pet that the owner has asked you not to do. Milo is a high-strung yet eager-to-please little fellow who won't assert himself if someone is scaring him. It's up to me to read his body language and tell a roughhousing guest that it's time to leave him alone. And nothing will get you barred from my house quicker than to reply to this request with, "No, look, he's enjoying it!" and continue on with rough play. Irritating one's hostess is not the most significant risk a person runs—frightened animals are dangerous animals, and you could get bitten or scratched.

When in any kind of doubt at all, *ask*. Ask before petting, and certainly ask before offering food. There are all kinds of human foods that are harmful to animals, and even harmless foods might be bad for a particular animal (they get food allergies, too). Especially, do not sneak little treats to a pet when you are being entertained at someone's home. For one thing, doing this can undo all the training the owner has tried to instill about not begging at the table. For another, other guests are probably doing the same thing. Sure, "just one little piece of cheese won't hurt him," but if each of the twelve dinner-party guests gives Max just one little piece of cheese, both Max and his owner are going to have a very unpleasant morning-after.

Introduce yourself

If you see an appealing, pettable-looking dog on the horizon, the first thing to do is to ask the owner if the dog is friendly. Not all dogs welcome being greeted by strangers. Make sure the tone of your voice implies that if the dog *isn't* friendly, you will not take this personally or judge the owner for it. Some dogs just don't like strangers. Perhaps they are skittish by nature, were abused by a former owner, or didn't receive enough socialization as puppies. So don't act as though the owner is somehow to blame for their dog's unsociability.

If the dog is a friendly one, the most natural-seeming thing to do is to pat it on the head, but don't. Dogs find that threatening, and if you think about how it looks from their angle, you can see why—it's like having the Death Star swooping in on you. Instead, put your hand out as a loose fist, with the back of your hand forward. Let the dog sniff you. Then just pay attention—the dog will tell you what it would like to do next. And don't ever put your face close to a strange dog's face, no matter how friendly the dog appears. Face-to-face intimacy doesn't mean in dog culture what it does in ours.

Now let's get down to business. If it is the appeal of the dog's *owner*, rather than the dog itself, that prompted your greeting, good doggie manners are even more crucial. Most dog owners have a vague mystical belief that their dogs are, in some deeply intuitive way, good judges of character. This is an irrational superstition with no basis in canine psychology whatsoever, but that's no reason not to use it to your advantage.* The best way to get a dog to like you is to squat down to talk to it. Few people

---

* Most dogs would abjectly worship O. J. Simpson if he had cheese in his pockets, and Leona Helmsley's Maltese, Trouble, undoubtedly loved her before it ever knew of that $12 million bequest.

do this, and while a good-natured dog will put up with being loomed over and patted on the head, they much prefer a person who's willing to get down on their level. So squat, already, thereby showing off your sculpted thighs as well as your compassion for the lower beasts. Present your hands for sniffing, and scratch the dog's throat and chest. You can tell the dog likes you if it sits down with its back to you—while rude in human terms, this is, literally, doggie language for "you got my back." If the dog then slowly slides down on its side and shows its belly—you're in. You're *so* in. This is when you know you can ask for a phone number, assuming you haven't already read it off the dog's tag.

Enough about manners for you—what about the animal? People are often neglectful about teaching proper greeting behavior to their dogs. Dogs that are inveterate jumpers should be kept leashed or crated when they're around anyone who might object to being jumped on. If you're dog-friendly, but don't care to be jumped on, ask the dog, "Can you *sit* so I can pet you?" Stress the word "sit" and the dog just might. The owner, at any rate, should get the message. If the owner is truly oblivious, back away and ask politely if she can call off her dog. If she says, "Oh, he's just being friendly" (the motto of clueless dog owners everywhere), respond with enthusiastic agreement, "Oh, I know!" and then repeat your request. It is possible to both acknowledge a dog's well-meaning intent and still not want it to jump on you. This is what you want to convey.

And then, alas, there's the sniffing. Dogs should be trained not to sniff people's crotches, and if a dog does, back off and ask the owner to pull the dog away. (If it helps with the embarrassment, keep in mind that sometimes a dog will go after your crotch not because that's where your private bits are, but because that's where your lap is and you may have spilled some food on it earlier.) Some general sniffing of legs, hands, and, if you're squatting, face, should be tolerated, if you're willing to tolerate dogs at all. Dogs lack the capacity for small talk, and giving you a good sniff-over is their way of getting answers to such questions as, "So, what do you do?" "How was your day?" and "Have you tried that new Indian place down the block yet?" It's unfair to deprive them of the most meaningful source of information they have.

One of the little idiosyncrasies of social life—amusing if you're in a generally good mood that day, annoying as hell if you're not—is that people complain constantly about the decline in good manners, yet when you try to teach good manners to your pet (or, for that matter, your children) it seems as though everyone leaps to reassure you that you don't need to. Don't be one of those people! If someone insists that his dog sit before being petted, don't even acknowledge the dog's presence until it is firmly down on its haunches.* It's hard enough to train dogs to restrain their natural instincts to lunge, lick, sniff, and beg. Dogs need consistency in order to learn, and well-meaning friends who "don't mind" being jumped on or who feed from the table can make a responsible owner's job much harder.

Interacting with cats is easier because cats are extremely clear about their boundaries. Like Midwesterners, dogs often feel obligated to be friendly even when they don't want to be. Like New Englanders, cats do not. If the cat wants to say hello, it will, and if it doesn't, you won't get within arm's reach of it. There is not much to be done about overly friendly cats except to try not to trip over them. If a cat is being truly obnoxious, ask its owner if

---

*Likewise, if a parent insists on "Mr." or "Ms." for adults, don't leap in with, "Oh, call me Jane!" The fact that being "Mrs. Smith" makes you feel old isn't important; supporting parents who are trying to teach their children manners is.

the cat, or the two of you, can move to another location for the duration of your visit. If you aren't a fan of cats, it's not a bad idea to promulgate the notion that you are allergic to them. Cat owners tend to respect this, and even see it as a sort of tribute to the Awesome Power of the Feline. (You can try the allergy excuse with dog owners, too, but sooner or later you'll run into a non-shedding poodle that you want to avoid, and then where will you be?)

If you are the guest of someone who has a pet more exotic than a dog or cat—a ferret, an iguana, a parrot—then ask the owner how to approach the animal, and do as they say. Almost all other animals are harder to read than dogs or cats, so obeying the owner's instructions is a matter of safety as well as etiquette.

Making friends with dog owners

In order to make friends with dog owners, especially if you meet them through their dogs, you're going to have to put up with a bit of dog talk. People who have pets like to talk about them, and people who don't aren't necessarily interested. Watch out for these common conversational pitfalls.

- **Don't judge the priorities of people who spend time or money on their pets.** I do not care to be lectured on how much time or money I spend on my dog by anyone who has ever drunk a beer or played a computer game. Yes, I do spend money on my dog when there are children going hungry in Africa. And I bet you own more than one pair of shoes, don't you? Unless you believe that no one has a right to luxuries until the planet has achieved economic justice for all—and you walk that walk yourself—don't criticize another person's discretionary spending.

- **Don't make snarky comments about the pets of childless people being "child substitutes."** If people really do see their pets that way, that is a tragic situation not to be made light of. If pets are the beloved companions of happily childless people, then they are not child substitutes, because no children are desired in the first place.

- **Don't dismiss the mourning that people go through when a pet dies.** Why would anyone do this? To prove the superior compassion and judgment of the human race? As a general principle it is not good etiquette, and even worse psychology, to assume that an emotion is somehow invalid or "made up" simply because you cannot relate to it. If someone tells you that they mourned more when their dog died than they did when their father passed away, assume that they have a good reason for that, express your condolences, and move on.

There's also good behavior, and the dynamic of pet talk isn't unique to pets, so it applies to a wide variety of situations. People who have diets, children, a personal relationship with the Lord, season tickets to the Sox, or a remodeling project also like to talk about their passions. And you may not share them.

Here's the thing: conversations take two. There are monomaniacal pet owners who simply will not shut up about Max or Sheba, ever. These people are annoying. However, whatever your interests are, tolerating a certain amount of pet (or food, child, God, Sox, or decorating) talk from others is only fair. Perhaps watching too much television has led us to believe that all conversations consist of witty banter punctuated by deep, soulful revelations. Thus, we feel that we are hard done by if we have to sit through the occasional monologue about Max's performance in agility class or how the new high-protein diet does away—really, it does, you should try it, it's amazing!—with the midafternoon slump.

Putting up with a certain amount of boredom gracefully is one of the responsibilities of a well-conducted life. If that boredom has gone well past a "certain amount," however, take control of the conversation and *make it* interesting. This doesn't mean hijacking the dialogue to your own set of interests; it means asking questions that enable you to be interested in what your conversational partner wants to talk about. If you like someone—or can gin up any positive emotion toward them at all, even if it's just morbid curiosity (an emotion not to be discounted, and which sometimes is as good as it gets with work colleagues and in-laws)—you can find some way to be interested in her perspective on things. If you can't, the problem is not with the other person for being boring—it's with you for being a childish narcissist who demands to be entertained at all times. Practice reciting Terence's catchphrase, "Nothing human is alien to me," and remember that in the realm of human endeavor, there's nothing we can't get interested in, at least for fifteen minutes.

When you're caught in a conversation with a person whose passions you don't share, here are ten good questions that will yield interesting-to-you answers about interests that you don't find intrinsically compelling:

1. What made you decide to [get a cat] [choose the beans-all-beans-naught-but-beans diet] [take up tantric meditation]?
2. What's been the biggest surprise?
3. What is the most important thing you've learned?
4. What advice would you give to anyone else who wanted

to [adopt a parrot] [build their own deck] [go on a weeklong fast]?

5. What kinds of people have you met at [the dog park] [the megachurch] [Home Depot]? How are they different from the non-[dog-owning] [religious] [home-owning] people you know?

6. What has been the biggest change in your life since you [got into tropical fish] [bought Red Sox season tickets] [had a child]?

7. How has [eating eighteen small meals a day] [finally having your own art studio] [converting to Islam] changed your relationship with your family/significant other?

8. What have you learned about yourself?

9. What's the biggest misconception people have about [cats] [the beans-all-beans-naught-but-beans diet] [tantric meditation]?

10. Who's the biggest name these days in [dog training] [interior decoration] [kabbalah]? What do you think of this person? Are they the real goods or just a celebrity?

Clearly, some of these questions are more personal than others and not appropriate in all situations. Still, you get the idea: take whatever topic you find boring *up* one level of abstractness. So Max's owner is all happy and glowy because she *thinks* she's talking about her beloved doggie, but she's actually discussing the nature of celebrity and why Cesar Millan got so popular, or dishing out wicked gossip on her neighbors, and that *is* interesting.

All human endeavors ultimately involve relationships, learning, problem solving, and ethics, four things that are intrinsically interesting to every scholar of the species.

Conclusion

THE PRINCIPLES OF THOUGHTFUL
ENGAGEMENT

Question: *Is etiquette relevant? It seems whether one is boarding the subway or working in business that our society has devolved to a "me first," "I've got mine," pushing and shoving match. Yes, I know etiquette is alive and well at the Four Seasons and among the Brahmin, but it seems like a bit of civilization that we lost in our efforts to make everything common.*

Do not confuse the two types of etiquette: basic Golden Rule–based kindness and the sort of formality that characterizes the Four Seasons and Boston Brahmins.* Mixing the two together is a categorical mistake. Common decency on one hand, and mas-

---

* Or so I imagine, anyway. I've never been to Four Seasons, and what with hanging out with a lot of science, technology, and academic folk, the Brahmins I know tend to be actual Indian Brahmins.

tery of the rituals of forks and calling cards on the other, both fall under the category of "manners" but are statistically independent of each other. In other words, you can be extremely adept at protocol and still be a nasty piece of work, and you can be a thoroughly kind and true soul who drinks out of the finger bowls.

Ideally, of course, you have both sorts of good manners. But common sense / decency etiquette is a matter of ethics, and forms/rituals etiquette is a matter of aesthetics. However polished their veneer, I suspect that "me first" and "I've got mine" attitudes are alive and well among the Boston Brahmins, and I believe the descendants of Irish immigrants to Boston would back me up on that.

The Slippery World of Fear and Freedom

"But as I travell'd hither through the land,
I find the people strangely fantasied;
Possess'd with rumours, full of idle dreams,
Not knowing what they fear, but full of fear:"

—*King John*, act 4, scene 2

If manners in both senses are getting worse, I think it's more interesting, and revealing, to look at the larger societal forces behind this than to go around blaming individuals. (Some of which I parsed in the introduction.) As the media balkanize into hundreds of TV channels and thousands of blogs, and the notion of a literary canon or a common source of information fades, our shared culture begins to erode. The less we have in common, the less we feel we owe one another. We are living in an anxious age. We are frightened of rising food and fuel prices, ecological catastrophe, losing our health insurance, losing our jobs, not having enough to retire on, the deficit, more war, more terrorism. A frightened animal is a dangerous animal; the human animal is no different. Then there's the fact that we live in an increasingly mobile society, making it difficult to forge the kind of long-term sense of place and community, and accountability, that has in the past served as a form of social control.

But here's the upside. People who bemoan the current state of today's manners—which can be pretty bad at times, I'm not denying that—are missing a crucial aspect: in the past forty years or so, for the first time in human history, *the modern West has signed on to the idea that courtesy should be extended to everybody.*

When you stop to think about it, the notion that everyone—regardless of nationality, religion, gender, occupation, race, age, or health status—should be treated with respect as an individual is extraordinary. I don't think we've ever tried that before, as a species. There were always classes of people—slaves and servants, women, children, the disabled, people of other nations, the poor—whom it was considered perfectly acceptable, even *moral*, to treat as less than human. We don't believe that anymore. Given the uniqueness and novelty of universal courtesy, it's hardly surprising that we're not very good at it. Yes, there is still prejudice. There is misogyny. There is racism. There is fat prejudice and discrimination against people with disabilities and homophobia and ageism and classism. But we acknowledge, at least with our conscious minds and in public, that these things are wrong. And people who engage in these behaviors have to entertain elaborate excuses for why what they are doing isn't *really* misogyny, racism, or the host of other prejudices. Even this represents progress.

The trend of modern society, albeit with fits and starts, is toward universal courtesy. Disability and illness aren't taken as a sign of God's wrath. Left-handed kids aren't whacked with rulers. Women are treated with respect because we are people, not because we belong to a man who is owed honor. It may not be universal yet—this kind of monumental change can't happen overnight or even within a generation—but the mere fact that the *ideal* of universal courtesy is accepted and not considered fecklessly utopian or an outright wicked assault on social order is itself astonishing.

Now when you're in the middle of an unprecedented social experiment, you're going to screw up. Even when we all agree that we should treat everyone with respect, we don't always know how to. Treating a pregnant woman with respect doesn't mean treating her like a man. Treating a disabled person with respect doesn't mean pretending he's not in a wheelchair. Treating a person of a different culture with respect doesn't mean making her an honorary American. Treating a broke friend with respect doesn't mean grousing about how much Uncle Sam takes out of everyone's taxes.

It's hard. We make mistakes. And it's possible that some people, overwhelmed, have unconsciously decided to throw in the towel. It's easier to give up on courtesy and focus on your own goals and needs than to try to be a good person when being good means figuring out so many things you never had to think about before and risk getting shot down when your intentions were innocent.

We also, as I've described in each of the book's chapters, have certain evolutionary tendencies that will make this social experiment an even more difficult one. It takes very little, for example, to get people thinking in terms of "us" and "them." You don't need centuries of festering history to get prejudiced, stereotyped thinking going—all you have to do is get a roomful of people to number off "one, two, one, two" and compete in a task. Within minutes, people will be thinking—and perhaps saying—"What a typical 'two' thing to do. Never trust a 'two'!" We are tribal thinkers. But we are *ethical* thinkers, as well.

I sometimes refer to the "Miss Conduct" column as advice on ethics, etiquette, and engineering. The basis of ethics is empathy, as embodied in the Golden Rule. The Jewish version is "That which is hateful to you, do not do unto others"; the Christian version is, "Do unto others as you would have them do unto you." These mirrored formulations—and all the other versions that have been devised—are based on the fundamental understanding that other people are like you, with desires, goals, loved ones, sorrows. A highly social species, humans have developed empathy to a degree unprecedented among other animals.

If we have ethics, do we really need *etiquette*? Isn't etiquette without ethics just meaningless form and ritual? Yes and no— form and ritual, yes; meaningless, no. Just because a lot of etiquette rules are random doesn't mean that they're pointless. Which side of the road you drive on is morally meaningless, too, but it's immensely helpful for everyone to agree on one side. The more rules you have for what you should wear to a wedding, how you should write a letter, and how you should eat artichokes, the fewer things you actually have to figure out on the fly. "Wait!" you say. Shouldn't we all live mindfully, taking in the fullness of every moment like William Blake after an est seminar? Oh, sure. But do you want to have a mindful encounter with your closet every time you get invited to someone's kid's bar mitzvah, or would you prefer simply to know that your dark gray business suit or blue jersey wrap dress are appropriate for all such occasions?

While engineers don't have a particularly good reputation for social skills, *engineering* can be a useful tool in the social maven's manners kit. Engineering is about arranging situations for people so that they do the "right" thing without thinking about it very hard. If you're worried about guests putting glasses down on the table, put cloths on them (the tables, I mean). If you think people will bring uninvited children to your wedding, go ahead and invite the kids and set up a nursery area. If your children don't like writing thank-you notes, break out the craft paper and glitter and craft it up, instead. These suggestions inevitably strike some people as dumbing down or compromising on "real etiquette." Fine. We all have areas where we feel the need to make a stand. But unless that clarion call is ringing in your soul, don't let the perfect be the enemy of the good.

And acknowledge that, no matter how ardent your ethics, charming your etiquette, or ingenious your engineering, others will criticize. Some people will think you're being a martinet by making your kids write thank-you notes at all; some people will be offended by the informality of the construction paper; others will find you unacceptably materialistic and wonder why you let people give your spoiled American brats presents, anyway, instead of requesting donations for the Sudan.

Let them. One price of living in a diverse society—a society where you are reasonably free to live according to your own values and preferences—is that people who make different choices than you will judge you. You are free to act; they are free to judge. That's how it works. You don't get to have both freedom to do as you wish and universal acclaim for it, unless you are Oprah. That's one price of freedom.

The other is that you will occasionally be impinged upon by others exercising their similar freedom. "Your right to swing your fist ends where my nose begins" is a lovely principle, but many things in life are less concrete than fists and noses. Atheists occasionally have to shut up, bow their heads, and keep a pleasant countenance while their hosts say grace before meals. Traditionalist married women must occasionally put up with being called "Ms." People who believe that money is a deeply private subject must occasionally put up with friends asking them how much they make. And people who dislike dogs, or animals in general, must put up with the fact that people will bring their animals anywhere they are legally permitted. You can get worked up over the fact that other people don't live their lives in a way designed to maximize your comfort and validate your choices, or you can get on with things.

So here I offer a final set of the seven principles for conducting yourself thoughtfully in this complicated world:

1. Acknowledge conflicting values.
2. Balance the real and the ideal.
3. Assume good intent.
4. Wear your ignorance gracefully.
5. Accept the inevitability of screwing up.
6. Err on the "right" side.
7. Realize that you always have a choice.

1. Acknowledge Conflicting Values

Choosing between right and wrong is, if not always easy, at least straightforward.

Choosing between one kind of "right" and another can be very difficult. Sometimes differences between people, even on petty matters, turn out to be driven by differences in values. Tim, who values privacy and propriety, was appalled when his friend Angie asked him how much he makes. Angie values openness, thinks secrecy about money undermines workers' power, and was offended that Tim thought she was rude. They hold conflicting values. As we have seen, the starting point for dealing with these kinds of conflicts is an acknowledgment that neither of them has the "right" value system. This acknowledgment doesn't point the way to a solution—that would be too easy and spoil all the fun. But it can put the situation in perspective. It's easier to treat people with respect when you understand that their behavior isn't driven by unthinking prejudice, habit, or inclination. Tim, who won't discuss his salary, isn't an uptight tool of The Man, any more than Angie was raised in a barn by folks who didn't know any better than to go around talkin' money. The issue for Tim and Angie isn't figuring out "who's right?" (the final two words of many of the questions that flurry across my e-mail), but negotiating a way of talking that feels honest and comfortable to both of them.

Just as frequently, individuals can find themselves torn between two conflicting values in their own minds.

Question: *What should you do when hosts prepare something for you that violates your principles or just disgusts you? While traveling in Hungary, a vegetarian friend and I had the rare opportunity to visit a Gypsy/Romany family. Our hostess made an elaborate show of offering us wine (okay), sliced cucumbers (okay), and black bread smeared with lard (not okay). We didn't know what to do to not offend her.*

Ah, the old problem of the nice vegetarian girl offered lard-smeared bread in a traditional Gypsy household. We've all been there. Choosing between vegetarianism and cross-cultural sharing is much harder than simply holding firm on your vegetarian ideals. The dilemma is especially hard when, because the lard platter is heading your way and there's no time to think, you are forced to decide *right now*—and, since you're traveling, you must communicate complex values in a foreign language or with gestures. So if certain comestibles threaten your very physical or spiritual existence—peanuts for the allergic, alcohol for the recovering, beef for the devout Hindu—prepare your excuse in advance. Learn to say "I'm sorry, I have an illness and can't have meat," or whatever, in the language of the countries you are visiting. Even if your reasons are ethical or religious, a health-related excuse is easier to explain and less judgmental sounding. (Plus, it's a neat party trick to be able to say "lactose-intolerant" in eleven languages.)

When you realize that a particular situation has you torn because two principles you value are in conflict, you are in a better position to assess your options. Which value is truly most important to you? Often, we choose a course of action because it is the least socially awkward thing to do in the moment, not because it reflects our deepest values or is what we would like to imagine ourselves doing. It's not awful to take the path of least resistance—but it should still be a conscious choice to do so. Finally, don't be stricter in the homes of others than you are in your own. Those of us who fall off the wagon occasionally because of our own lack of willpower should be willing to fall off occasionally in the name of friendship, as well.

Let's say, for example, that our vegetarian heroine ate the lard. As she saw the dread plate bearing down on her, she summoned the will to dismiss her long-held food scruples in order to reach out to the Romany (who are, after all, one of the most misunderstood and mistreated minority groups on the planet).

Had she done this, she probably wouldn't have experienced much guilt afterward. Even if she had—if she had decided, later on, that she'd made the wrong choice—it still would have been a choice, and one based on an ethical principle. If, on the other hand, she panicked in the heat of the moment and downed the bread in a compulsive seizure of social conformity, she probably would have reproached herself later. In that situation, she would have betrayed her vegetarian principles without actively choosing the virtue of graciousness (and probably without even enjoying the bread and the lard, which I've heard is quite tasty if you can get over the idea of it).

2. Balance the Real and the Ideal

As an advice columnist, I try not to judge the values of the people who write to me. I have my private opinions, certainly, but my job is to help people live up to their *own* values in the most considerate and least crazy-making way possible. This often translates into recommending a compromise, as I did for our vegetarian friend by suggesting she follow her beliefs, but not aggressively evangelize for them. I recommended this because she described a situation in which compromise was possible, and in which it didn't seem reasonable to try to make a moral case for vegetarianism. (Cultural differences aside, it wasn't even clear if she and her hosts spoke the same language.)

Compromise isn't always possible or desirable. There are times when you have to take a stand in order to be able to face yourself afterward. This doesn't mean getting self-righteous and shouting "I am Spartacus!" Calm self-assertion, leavened with a sense of humor, works just as well—even better, really, because it doesn't spark an equal flame of self-righteous indignation on the other side of your relationship conflict.

On the other hand, sometimes you should give in. Not every preference we hold dear represents a value. Some are merely the behavioral equivalent of fashion statements. There is a difference between a sixty-year-old Hindu whose lips have never touched beef and a college sophomore who has been vegan since the beginning of the semester. There is a difference between people who allow their ethical scruples to inconvenience only themselves and those who allow their scruples to inconvenience other people. It's thoughtful and gracious to willingly put yourself out for the sake of others. Paradoxically, there are situations in which choosing to go against a moral principle can elevate your moral status. If I knew that a vegetarian friend had deliberately chosen to eat pork lard in order to show respect to Gypsies, I would probably be very impressed with her compassion and sturdy digestion, and be inclined to give her moral intuitions a lot of weight thereafter.

When ethical matters are at stake, only the individual concerned can decide how serious the issue is and whether conviction, compromise, or caving in is most appropriate. Those of us who are not saints cannot live out each ethical principle to its fullest in every moment of the day. Rather, because time and energy are finite, most people have a few pet values (virtues, ideals, causes) into which they pour their energy: sometimes you Save This Child, sometimes you turn the page. Calvin may be a superb father but a standoffish neighbor; Kathleen may devote time and money to animal rescue shelters but do little for the environment, even though she believes it is important.

If other people's ethical balance sheets aren't quite the same as your own, it doesn't necessarily mean they lack values, just that they are allocating their limited time, money, and energy in a different way. As the Pirkei Avot, an ancient text of Jewish wisdom, states, "It is not upon you to complete the task, but you are not free to desist from it." The task referred to is that of repairing, or perfecting, the world. I find this a helpful saying to meditate on: we must all do *something*, but no one needs, or can, do *everything*. Therefore, try to avoid quibbling with the ethical priorities of others or laying guilt trips on them because their causes are not your own. They are tending to their gardens, and you to yours.

3. Assume Good Intent

Have you ever tried to have a conversation with someone whom you were convinced was stupid or evil? How did that work out? Probably not well; most people get remarkably defensive when asked to consider the depth of their stupidity or evil, no matter how politely the request is phrased.

So don't try. Rather, no matter how absurd a person's words or actions may seem to be, assume that their intentions are good. They may know things that you don't or have had experiences that lead them to react in certain ways. Or they may be completely ignorant of facts that are evident to everyone else. But they do, most likely, mean to act for the best.

This is something I learned in acting class: no one ever believes he or she is a villain. One of the first things you learn about playing a bad guy is that you can't play him as though he *thinks* he's a bad guy. If you do, you'll just be doing mustache-twirling silliness. No, even the worst characters are convinced that they are acting reasonably and with good faith. *King Lear's* Goneril and Regan don't see themselves as ungrateful vipers but as ordinary people driven beyond the limits of patience by an erratic and tyrannical father. The murderous Macheath of *The Threepenny Opera* sees himself not as an exploiter and murderer but as a man who is simply more honest about his desires, and the methods he employs to satisfy them, than the rest of us.

A wonderful book by Douglas Stone, Bruce Patton, and Sheila Heen, *Difficult Conversations: How to Discuss What Matters Most*, discusses *how* to assume good intent. The authors recommend that we "disentangle intent from impact" when other people have offended us. In other words, just because your feelings are hurt, your plans are disrupted, or your philodendron is killed doesn't mean that the person who insulted your fiancé, dropped in unannounced on the dinner party you were having, or volunteered to house-sit and then forgot to water the upstairs greenery *intended* to have the effect she did.

Does this mean that you must simply bury your hurt feelings and dead philodendron, and, sighing "They meant well," take up the mantle of victimhood? Of course not. But you can stand up for yourself much better when you discuss the facts of the situation rather than going on the attack about why your irresponsible friend let your poor Philly die. You'll be less emotional, for one thing. For another, people can argue endlessly about motives and circumstances, but outside of a *Monty Python* sketch no one can debate the objective existence of a dead philodendron.

Sometimes, too, the assumption of good intent can be a nifty rhetorical trick to let people know that they've overstepped a boundary of kindness and good sense. You *know* they didn't mean to hurt you, so why on earth would they say these things? This is especially useful when well-meaning folks insult you. For example, people often say the most amazing things when other people tell them what they do for a living:

"I'M A LAWYER."	*"How can you stand that?"*
"I'M A PSYCHOLOGIST."	*"Isn't psychology mostly common sense?"*
"I'M IN ADVERTISING."	*"Work for the dark side, do you?"*
"I'M A WAITRESS."	*"That's funny, you seem so bright."*

And, of course,

"I'M A STAY-AT-HOME MOM."	*"Don't you get bored?"*

As a rejoinder to such shortsighted conversation, don't storm off offended or leap into an impassioned defense of your chosen profession. Instead, open your eyes wide and ask the person, "I love what I do, but I'm curious—do you normally insult the career of someone you've just met?" Then sit back and enjoy the stammers until your thirst for vengeance is satisfied (it shouldn't take longer than thirty seconds or so) and then begin explaining some of the joys of child raising, litigation, or the like.

4. Wear Your Ignorance Gracefully

I know one thing about you: you are unbelievably ignorant. So am I. Here is a brief list of the things I do not know: what the periodic table of the elements actually *means*; how to make a white sauce, or, for that matter, why; the cause of the Hundred Years' War; the *length* of the Hundred Years' War;* why *Moby-*

---

* I'm guessing a hundred years, but it could be one of those trick questions.

Dick is such a great book; how Christians figure out when Easter is; the rules of football; and pretty much anything at all about China except that it is very large and very important. As a good friend of mine once put it, I'm "astronomically ignorant." He meant that he didn't know anything about astronomy, but the statement works however you choose to read it.

Please don't offer to educate me, especially about the rules of football. My point is that even the most well-informed, educated person imaginable has vast, unsown tracts of ignorance in their brain. I could make a larger argument that it is not really possible to be an educated person today, as it was perhaps a hundred years ago, when a person could legitimately feel that he or she had a decent grip on everything worth knowing. Today, the sciences have made such strides that it is difficult even for professionals to keep up within their subspecialties, let alone matters outside them, and the humanities have opened their doors to works by women, people of color, non-Westerners, and other such folks who used to be kept out of the canon. This is fair and right, of course, but it does make it rather hard to sustain the illusion that you've read everything worth reading. All of which is to say that, as a marvelous *New Yorker* cartoon had it, "It's all right, sweetie. In the information age, everybody feels stupid."

All of this sociology, though, should help you realize that you should never be surprised by another person's ignorance nor embarrassed to admit your own. It is difficult to admit when we don't know something, but as they say about aging, the alternative is worse: in this case, pretending to know something you don't. (There is a difference between ignorance and stupidity: an ignorant person may not know something, but a stupid person doesn't *know* he doesn't know, and doesn't think that it is important to know.)

When you admit your own ignorance, you free other people from being ashamed of what they don't know—and if everyone can admit what they do and don't know, then maybe real learning can happen. Psychologists have identified a phenomenon called "pluralistic ignorance," which is when everyone assumes that everyone else knows what's going on, and therefore doesn't ask any questions for fear of revealing their ignorance. "Everyone else," of course, is as ignorant as our original "everyone," and equally embarrassed to speak up.* In an environment of pluralistic ignorance, everyone muddles on, a little army of the perplexed, each one of whom is certain that his ignorance is uniquely shameful and must be concealed at all costs.

Yes, of course, it sounds like every meeting you've ever been to in your life. Social psychology has all kinds of wonderful concepts like that; read a textbook on the topic, and you'll swear those researchers had bugged your company's conference room. But what does facing up to the inevitability of ignorance have to do with dealing with a diverse society? Quite a bit, actually. Because when you face up to your ignorance, you can start asking questions, and when you start asking questions, you can engage people with different priorities from a position of genuine curiosity. You do want to make sure your questions don't come across as patronizing ("Tell me of your quaint customs, o charming native!") or as passive-aggressive editorializing ("But won't Joshua be awfully lonely as an only child?"). The best way to do this isn't by watching your words obsessively—that will only lead to self-consciousness.

---

* This is why, after a talk, it is better to ask, "What questions do you have?" than "Any questions?" People often won't admit to not understanding something, but if they believe that questions are expected, they'll pipe up.

Instead, try to cultivate an attitude of genuine interest in the other person. If your main motive is to discover, rather than to convert, you will instinctively ask the right questions.

And when you are unashamed to ask questions, you don't have to guess what to do in ambiguous situations—and there are a lot of ambiguous situations out there. I sometimes get the impression that some of my readers believe there is a Right Answer for every situation and they are expected to know it, and that admitting they don't know it (to anyone but my million or so readers and me, that is) would be terribly shameful. Usually I find myself explaining to these people that no, in fact, I don't know the Right Answer either, and if they want to find it out, they'd better ask the person who put them in the situation to begin with. If your brother is marrying his male partner of twenty years and asks you to plan a bachelor party for him, you don't need to figure out, all on your own, what a bachelor party for a gay man who's been in a committed relationship for two decades should be like. Just ask him what he wants. If a foreign coworker pronounces her name with a trilled "r," and some people in your office do and some don't, ask her which pronunciation she prefers. You don't need to be a mind reader to be kind and considerate—just willing to ask.

5. Accept the Inevitability of Screwing Up

Though teachers may claim otherwise, there is indeed such a thing as a stupid question—and a correspondingly infinite array of stupid comments, thoughts, and actions to go along with them. And anyone who doesn't occasionally commit random acts of stupidity probably ought to start taking a few more chances in life.

Social mistakes are inevitable. They always have been, because even the most conformist of people are an unpredictable and idiosyncratic lot. In a more diverse society, in which rules are in flux, social mistakes are—well, there isn't anything more inevitable than "inevitable," but if there were, that's what they would be.

People often have the idea that etiquette is about never making mistakes. Mistake! Just as yoga is not about maintaining perfect balance but constantly *regaining* your footing, so, too, the practice of etiquette is not about achieving a state of frozen perfection but about equilibrium, awareness, and the ability to get back on your feet, even if one of them is currently in your mouth.

When you accept that mistakes are inevitable:

- **You can take chances.** In the early 1970s, psychologist Phil Zimbardo conducted the infamous "Stanford Prison Experiment," in which two dozen young middle-class men were randomly assigned to roles as "prisoners" and "guards" in a makeshift jail in the basement of the Stanford psychology building. (No, participating in such social experiments aren't the kind of chances I think you should take. Bear with me. We'll get there.) Within hours, the men had become completely identified with their prisoner or guard roles—prisoners becoming withdrawn, rebellious, or depressed, and guards becoming sadistic bullies.

  Zimbardo cut his planned two-week experiment short after six days, and there is still controversy over whether he should have let the experiment go on that long—or if he ever should have conducted it in the first place. The experiment is best known today for its power to explain the brutality that ordinary people are capable of when they are given power over others. But the psychological dynamics in that makeshift basement "prison" suggested something else to Zimbardo as well: the experience of shyness.

Some people are shy all the time, and almost everyone is shy under some circumstances (speaking in public, for example, or going to a party where most of the guests are strangers). Whether a person is shy as a permanent personality trait or as a temporary state brought about by external circumstances, the experience is much the same: essentially, that of a little Stanford prison right there in the shy person's head. When you feel shy, it's the inner guard shouting at you that your contributions are worthless, that no one has respect or regard for you—and it's the inner prisoner who curls into a ball in the corner of the cell. Shyness, according to Zimbardo and his collaborator Lynn Henderson, is "a self-imposed prison of silence and solitary confinement."

When you accept that mistakes are inevitable and not a cause for exile from the human race, the guard in your head loses a lot of power. "You'll screw up!" he yells, and you retort, "So?" And the prison doors open. You can be free to ask the questions you're curious about or introduce yourself to a stranger. You can commit all those random acts of kindness and senseless acts of beauty that bumper stickers have been urging you to do over the years. You can take advantage of each day's wealth of opportunities to comfort, inform, or amuse other people or yourself, knowing that failure isn't death. Sometimes your efforts will pay off, sometimes they won't. Confidence doesn't mean believing that all your comments will be welcome and your jokes laughed at—it means believing that you can survive if they're not.

And you *will* survive your mistakes. Perhaps you'll even be better liked on account of them. A less disturbing series of psychological experiments showed, unsurprisingly, that people prefer articulate and well-groomed folks to scruffy mutterers. However, they liked articulate and well-groomed folks *who spilled coffee on themselves* best of all. Apparently we're all a bit shy, and seeing a little flaw in someone else goes a long way toward making others comfortable. Haven't you ever been delighted when someone admits that they've forgotten your name, because you've forgotten theirs as well? And don't we all know that warm glow that comes when someone *else* forgets to attach a document to an e-mail, just as we so often do?

- **You can forgive yourself.** If you do something worse than spill a little coffee—ask a non-pregnant woman when her baby is due, for example—you can forgive yourself. "Forgiving yourself," unfortunately, has awful self-indulgent connotations of drowning in a sea of self-love and affirmations. I don't mean that, quite the opposite. Forgiving yourself means *not* focusing on yourself and the mistake you made, but instead leaping over that wallow of self-blame quickly enough that you can make sure no one else's feelings were hurt or plans inconvenienced by your boo-boo, and fixing whatever damage was done as best you can. Chances are that if you have generally treated a person with respect and consideration, they will be willing to give you a few "Get Out of Jail Free" cards, and give you credit for good intentions even when you've done or said something truly stupid.

- **You can forgive others.** Those "Get Out of Jail Free" cards—you'll want to collect them and trade them with your friends. If someone wishes you Merry Christmas instead of Happy Hanukkah, forgets to ask if you have any allergies or ethical concerns before inviting you to dinner, or doesn't think to ask about your new baby— well, sure, maybe they're an anti-Semitic child hater hoping to poison you with peanuts. Or perhaps they're just deeply overwhelmed by the attempt to keep track of the culinary, career, religious, family, health, and leisure issues of everyone they know.

As with assuming good intent, being willing to let go of other people's mistakes doesn't mean being a willing victim. If your friend *still* cannot remember after a dozen dinners together that you are allergic to peanuts and cannot eat his famous Satay à la Jif, speak up. But don't yell. (Haven't you ever forgotten something twelve times?) Research shows that people who feel psychologically safe can admit to errors and learn from them. People who believe that they will be attacked, on the other hand, become defensive and refuse to acknowledge mistakes. Acknowledging errors is a very unnatural thing to do—it requires us to suppress our instinct to protect our self-image. By not embarrassing others—by showing them through your attitude that mistakes are normal—you can create a situation in which people can focus on repairing their relationship with you rather than repairing their own self-image.

6. Err on the "Right" Side

Though mistakes are inevitable, not all mistakes are created equal. A man who is discreet to a fault risks being considered aloof. A man who is indiscreet to a fault risks having compromising photos of himself surface when a potential romantic partner or employer Googles him on the Internet. Not all mistakes bear equal consequences. Because of this, it's a good idea, in a new or ambiguous situation, to assess the kinds of mistakes you could possibly make and then make the best ones.

This notion came to me, coincidentally enough, when I was interviewing to write the "Miss Conduct" column for the *Boston Globe*. Doug Most, the editor of the Sunday magazine section, told me that I should err on the side of being too edgy or idiosyncratic in my writing. If the editors didn't have to rein me in on occasion, he said, I probably wasn't doing my job right.

I thought this was damn smart. Doug knew that it would take me some time to hit my stride, as it would for anyone taking over a new job. And he knew that, as an editor, it's easier to tell a writer to tone a piece down than to tell her to give it more flavor. Of course, if the creative product is a casserole rather than a column, it's easier to add flavor than remove it. A wise cook will err on the side of putting too little spice or salt in rather than too much. Judge which mistake is worse by what situation you are in.

The newsroom and kitchen aren't the only places the "err on the right side" principle is useful. As mentioned above, erring on the side of discretion is usually wise. If you think you've been standoffish, you can always warm up later on (which often charms people more, because they think they've won you over). But if you've impulsively told your jogging partner about the time you danced to "I'm Too Sexy" on a tabletop, dressed only in an adult diaper and Mickey Mouse ears, as part of a fraternity initiation, you will never be able to erase the image seared on his brain.

An often-overlooked point about discretion is that it goes two ways. You can offer other people the chance to be discreet by not making assumptions about them. This is why being wished "Merry Christmas" can be annoying to non-Christians. Ahmed would like to treat his religion as a private matter, but when Caitlin wishes him a Merry Christmas, he feels he must either be untrue to himself by smiling and saying "Merry Christmas," or play Spokesman for His People, piping up with, "Actually, I am Muslim, but I will certainly enjoy my day off, and I hope you have a wonderful Christmas." That may not be a role Ahmed wishes to play that day.

In these days of changing standards, erring on the side of formality is also usually a safe choice (especially in a business context)—offering formal respect to others, that is, rather than demanding it for yourself. People who prefer informality are rarely downright offended by more formal manners, but those who prefer the old-school style can get their backs up in a hurry. Stick with honorifics in business correspondence, salutations and sign-offs in e-mails, and "Sir" and "Ma'am" when dealing with strangers—at least until other norms are established as the relationship progresses. You'll cause delight in the hearts of many and wonderment in the minds of more.

Discretion and formality are general principles—more specifically, it's a kind and generous thing to err on the side of overtipping and writing thank-you notes even if they aren't specifically called for.

7. Realize That You Always Have a Choice

A choice? What am I saying? In any social situation you usually have *dozens* of choices. It may not seem that way in the heat of the moment, but it's true. When I was teaching, I would occasionally do a classroom exercise called "Get the Grail." I would hold up some object—the grail—and tell the students to imagine that this object was the key to all their greatest desires: love, fame, happiness, money, an "A" in the class. They were to use any method short of physical violence to get me to give them the grail. (Anyone who did something I thought particularly effective got the grail. I gave away little prizes to keep it interesting.)

Students could be wonderfully inventive in this exercise. They would bribe, threaten, cajole, and distract me. They worked alone and in teams. They sang and danced. They spoke in foreign languages and told long complicated stories. They made reasoned arguments. Occasionally, someone would simply stand very close to me and say, "Give me the grail. Give me the grail. Give me the grail. Give me the grail"—over and over in a monotone until I handed it over just to shut him up.

The point of "Get the Grail" wasn't only to amuse the teacher, although, of course, it always did. The point was to get people to realize how many ways there are to accomplish a goal and to make them think about what kinds of strategies they used—in real life as well as in a silly classroom game. Did they have a lot of strategies or just one? Did they pay attention to what worked and what didn't and refine their tactics accordingly? Or did they keep on with whatever they were doing, regardless of my response?

Your Mind, Our Manners

"The only place different social types can genuinely get along with each other is in heaven."

—J.D., *Heathers*

J.D. has a point. It is extraordinarily difficult for different social types to get along. The topics covered in this book are of deep, existential importance to us. Can you imagine not having children, if you do? Loving cats, if you don't? Worshipping God, if you don't? Being straight, if you're gay? Eating *real* Chinese food for the rest of your life if you grew up in Minneapolis? Chances are good that these changes don't come across as small things to contemplate: any one of them would fundamentally alter the fabric of your being. So it's no wonder that people whose values, priorities, and experiences differ from yours in these basic ways can seem, at times, almost alien.

And sometimes our differences seem all too familiar—which can be even more slippery. Many of our choices have ambivalence to them. Even the most happily married person occasionally misses the freedom of her single days. Even the most career-driven professional would like on occasion to chuck it all and become a beachcomber. Even the most ardent locavore is occasionally attracted by the whiff of McDonald's french fries. That ambivalence within our own souls—we can so easily project it onto others. Many of the choices we make represent an argument we've had with some part of ourselves. When we see another person who made the opposite choice, we're afraid that she might awaken the part of us that lost the argument and therefore introduce conflict into our lives. Often, out of an instinct of self-protection, we go on the attack.

But we can stop. We can own our choices, our experiences, our values, and our priorities and still retain empathy for others; still maintain some basic rituals and forms for a changing world that will help us not to have to figure out every situation from the ground up; and still figure out clever workarounds for potentially awkward situations.

We're cave people, living in a complicated world. It's not natural to be courteous to everyone, to treat the stranger with respect. But let's keep working on it. Because if we can pull this universal courtesy thing off, *if we can let our minds rule over our manners*, we are going to be one freaking amazing species.

And, yes, that's the scientific term.

A Note to the Reader

Life is full of misunderstandings, missteps, and awkward encounters: You sent a gift to someone, but the recipient never said thank you. Wracked by angst over whether your friend received the gift, you debate whether to ask and risk making your friend appear ungrateful. Or perhaps you don't want to evenly split a restaurant tab if you've had only a salad. Should you pay less and look like a cheapskate?

Miss Conduct is here to help. If you have a question, or even an etiquette tip to share, e-mail missconduct@globe.com. Your question and Miss Conduct's answer may appear in a future issue of the the *Boston Globe Magazine*.

Appendix

RECIPES FOR THE SOUL

*Miss Conduct's Kosher, Halal, High-Protein,
Low-Carb, Budget Soul Food Buffet for
Guests with Multiple Food Allergies*

*Baked chicken drumsticks à la Denise
Collard greens with black beans or lentils
Vegetarian dirty rice
Baked squash and tofu
Corn muffins
Salad*

This is a good buffet dinner to serve when you are dealing with a lot of different food rules. Only one dish has meat and one has eggs and dairy (the corn muffins). There is no wheat and minimal sugar. It can be made either kosher or halal, but check with your guests in advance to find out how strict their level of observance is.

Baked chicken drumsticks à la Denise
1 package chicken drumsticks
1 cup olive oil
1 head of garlic—half the cloves coarsely chopped, half
    smashed
Seasoning (Cavender's Greek Seasoning, Mrs. Dash, or other
    seasoning mix)
2 tbsp. lemon juice

Wash drumsticks. Place in baking dish. Make a marinade out of the oil, lemon juice, seasoning, and smashed garlic and pour it over drumsticks. Rub the marinade into the drumsticks with your hands. Really work it in! Insert the chopped garlic under the chicken skin. Cover in foil and marinate overnight, turning once. Cook for 3 hours at 300 degrees, removing foil for last hour. Let cool before serving.

Collard greens with black beans or lentils
3 tbsp. vegetable or peanut oil
1 large onion, chopped
1 clove of garlic, chopped fine
1 large or two small bunch collard greens
1 15-oz. can black beans or lentils, drained
Salt and pepper (to taste)
Maple syrup and/or hot sauce

Heat oil in pan until shimmering. Add garlic and onion and sauté over medium heat for approximately 7 minutes or until onion is translucent. Wash collard greens, remove biggest stems, and roll the leaves up tight together, then slice crosswise into thin ribbons. Add to pan and cook until dull green, stirring frequently. Add beans or lentils and continue heating. Add salt and pepper. Drizzle with maple syrup, if desired, or else serve with maple syrup and hot sauce and let guests choose.

Vegetarian dirty rice
4 tbsp. olive oil
1 onion (red or yellow), diced
1 clove of garlic, minced
1 tsp. each basil, oregano, chili powder, paprika
2 cups brown rice
4 cups water or vegetable stock
1 15-oz. can diced tomatoes (with juice)
3 or 4 stalks celery, sliced thin
1 or 2 carrots, diced
1 bell pepper, whichever color you think is prettiest, diced

Heat oil in large saucepan or Dutch oven. Sauté onion and garlic until translucent or caramelized, depending on how patient you are. Add seasonings and rice. Sauté rice for 3 minutes, stirring occasionally. Add vegetables and broth and stir it all up. Bring to a boil for 5 minutes, then reduce the heat, cover the pan, and let simmer for 20–25 minutes or until liquid is evaporated.

Baked squash and tofu
1 14-oz. block extra-firm tofu
Half a butternut squash, skinned and seeded
Olive oil spray
Cumin, coriander, and chili powder (for a spicy version)

Pumpkin pie spice mix or cinnamon, allspice, and cardamom
(for a sweeter version)
Hot sauce (optional)

Drain tofu and pat dry. Cut tofu and squash into ½-inch cubes.
Spray olive oil on a nonstick baking sheet (a silicone baking sheet
that you put over a regular cookie sheet is great) and put the
squash and tofu cubes down in a single layer. Sprinkle with
spices. Cook for about 40 minutes at 350 degrees, turning once
or twice. A fork should go easily through the squash, and the tofu
should be slightly crisp on the outside.

Serve with hot sauce on the side for those who like a little
kick with their beta-carotene.

Corn muffins
These can be made from a packaged mix and, at my house, you
know they are. Check the package if you have vegetarians or
kosher-keepers coming over, as some brands have animal short-
ening. Note: corn muffins are not vegan friendly.

Salad
Since most of this meal has complex flavors, get the simplest
salad greens you can, either mixed spring greens, romaine, or
Boston lettuce. These are best served with a plain oil and vinegar
dressing.

Bibliography

IMPROVE YOUR MIND OVER MANNERS

Interested in reading more? Here are some books on the topics covered in *Miss Conduct's Mind over Manners*. This isn't by way of being a formal bibliography—take it more in the spirit of recommendations from a friend. Should you ever run into one of my actual friends, they will verify that I do in fact recommend these books, quite vociferously.

Barry Schwartz and other behavioral economists have written about "the paradox of choice"—the fact that the more options one is presented with, the harder it becomes to make a decision, and the less satisfied you are with what you eventually choose. So I've decided to list only three or four books for each topic, in the hopes that you might actually read some of them.

General

Bishop, Bill. *The Big Sort: Why the Clustering of Like-Minded America Is Tearing Us Apart* (New York: Houghton Mifflin Co., 2008).

Putnam, Robert. *Bowling Alone: The Collapse and Revival of American Community* (New York: Simon & Schuster, 2000).

Post, Peggy. *Emily Post's Etiquette, 17th Edition* (New York: Collins Living, 2004).

Stone, Douglas, Bruce Patton, and Sheila Heen. *Difficult Conversations: How to Discuss What Matters Most* (New York: Penguin, 2000).

Tocqueville, Alexis de. *Democracy in America* (New York: Penguin Classics, 2003).

Food

Chen, Joanne. *The Taste of Sweet: Our Complicated Love Affair with Our Favorite Treats* (New York: Crown, 2008).

Pollan, Michael. *The Omnivore's Dilemma* (New York: Penguin, 2006).

Wansink, Brian. *Mindless Eating: Why We Eat More Than We Think* (New York: Bantam Books, 2007).

Money

Ariely, Dan. *Predictably Irrational: The Hidden Forces That Shape Our Decisions* (New York: Harper, 2008).

Greenhouse, Steve. *The Big Squeeze: Tough Times for the American Worker* (New York: Alfred A. Knopf, 2008).

Kasser, Tim. *The High Price of Materialism* (Cambridge, Mass.: MIT Press, 2002).

Schor, Juliet. *The Overspent American: Why We Want What We Don't Need* (New York: HarperPerennial, 1999).

Religion

Farkas, Steve, et al. *For Goodness' Sake: Why So Many Want Religion to Play a Greater Role in American Life* (New York: Public Agenda, 2001).

Horgan, John. *Rational Mysticism: Spirituality Meets Science in the Search for Enlightenment* (New York: Houghton Mifflin, 2004).

Radosh, Dan. *Rapture Ready: Adventures in the Parallel Universe of Christian Pop Culture* (New York: Scribner, 2008).

Wolfe, Alan. *The Transformation of American Religion: How We Actually Live Our Faith* (Chicago: University of Chicago Press, 2005).

Sex and Relationships

Etcoff, Nancy. *Survival of the Prettiest: The Science of Beauty* (New York: Anchor, 2000).

Hochschild, Arlie, and Arlene Machung. *The Second Shift* (New York: Penguin, 2003).

Kanter, Rosabeth Moss. *Men and Women of the Corporation: New Edition* (New York: Basic Books, 1993).

Wallerstein, Judith, and Sandra Blakeslee. *The Good Marriage: How and Why Love Lasts* (New York: Grand Central Publishing, 1996).

Children

Bloom, Paul. *Descartes's Baby: How the Science of Child Development Explains What Makes Us Human* (New York: Basic Books, 2005).

Coontz, Stephanie. *The Way We Really Are: Coming to Terms with America's Changing Families* (New York: Basic Books, 1998).

Crittenden, Ann. *The Price of Motherhood: Why the Most Important Job in the World Is Still the Least Valued* (New York: Holt Books, 2002).

Peskowitz, Miriam. *The Truth Behind the Mommy Wars: Who Decides What Makes a Good Mother?* (Berkeley, California: Seal Press, 2005).

Health

Goffman, Erving. *Stigma: Notes on the Management of Spoiled Identity* (New York: Touchstone, 1986).

Groopman, Jerome. *How Doctors Think* (New York: Mariner, 2008).

Harding, Kate, and Marianne Kirby. *Lessons from the Fat-o-sphere: Quit Dieting and Declare a Truce with Your Body* (New York: Perigee Trade, 2009).

Salamon, Julie. *Hospital: Man, Woman, Birth, Death, Infinity, Plus Red Tape, Bad Behavior, Money, God and Diversity on Steroids* (New York: Penguin Press, 2008).

Pets

Budiansky, Stephen. *The Truth About Dogs: An Inquiry into the Ancestry, Social Conventions, Mental Habits, and Moral Fiber of* Canis Familiaris (New York: Penguin Group, 2000).

Grandin, Temple, and Catherine Johnson. *Animals in Translation: Using the Mysteries of Autism to Decode Animal Behavior* (New York: Harvest Books, 2006).

Shevelow, Katherine. *For the Love of Animals: The Rise of the Animal Protection Movement* (New York: Henry Holt & Co., 2008).

Acknowledgments

I tried to combine generosity with common sense
wherever possible and nobody can accuse me of not
having done my best.
>   —Robert Graves, *Claudius the God*

How dreadfully intimidating for an etiquette columnist to
have to write an extremely public thank-you note! I risk all
credibility should my memory or turn of phrase fail me. Never-
theless, as I so often advise others: overcome self-consciousness
and soldier on.

I owe so much to so many people for this project. In a way,
it is a culmination of my long and winding professional and
personal career; it wouldn't be out of place to simply say,
"Thank you to everyone I have ever met." But that would hardly
be fair to those who deserve a special place of honor.

First off, thanks to everyone who helped to make me, officially, "Miss Conduct," and thereby helped this book to come into
existence. Thanks to Mark Kramer, whose narrative journalism
conference was the right place that I happened to be at that right
time some five years ago, and who provided me with valuable
advice when I took the gig. Editor Susanne Althoff was at that

conference, and had the imagination to look outside the ranks of etiquette consultants and allow this psychologist, drama geek, and stand-up comic to audition for the job. Susanne is the Colonel Parker to my Elvis, the Brian Epstein to my John Lennon, the Malcolm McLaren to my Sid Vicious, and I would be nothing without her. Doug Most created the *Boston Globe Magazine* in its current form, including the "Miss Conduct" column, and has provided steady leadership. Attorney Sean Ploen looks after my interests and advises me on etiquette issues related to intellectual property (there's more than you'd think). Agent Dan O'Connell shepherded this book through the second-longest awkward stage in the history of human development. Robin Dennis is the kind of book editor people don't think exists anymore—learned, sympathetic, insightful, thorough.

A book that purports to be on diversity will of necessity need input from other folks besides the writer. Catherine Caldwell-Harris has been an invaluable sounding board and conversational partner and has helped me to keep up to date on the latest psychological research. Dany Spencer Adams and Verena Weiloch, likewise, have spent many hours unraveling knotty problems and knitting up the raveled sleeves of care with me, for which I thank them (and thanks to Verena also for proofreading and offering suggestions to improve my recipes—not just the ones in this book, either). Thanks to bloggers Kate Harding, Fillyjonk, and Sweet Machine at kateharding.net; PeaceBang; BostonGal; Muslimah Media Watch; Surviving the Workday; and Melissa McEwan and the gang at Shakespeare's Sister for the multiple perspectives they provide, and thanks to their readers and commenters. Denise Spiliotis provided the recipe for Greek baked drumsticks and various other forms of inspiration. Thanks to

Darcy Davidson, author of the original Craigslist Cancer Rant, and all the other ranters who wrote in to my blog. My friend who wanted to buy my other friend a beer never got the opportunity, but I'll buy him one someday and he'll never know why. Thanks to the Wellesley Mothers' Forum and the Peabody Essex Museum for giving me a lively venue to discuss some of my ideas, and to Peaco Todd and the Powder Point Avenue gang for providing peace and quiet in which the first draft got completed.

Every now and then, you make a choice that affects everything else. For me, it was moving to Boston. Sigmund Freud said the important things in life were work and love—Alfred Adler added friendship to the list. Boston has provided me more than I could have hoped for in all those domains. Professionally, I will always be indebted to Richard Ely, Jean Berko Gleason, and Robert Harrison, the world's most harmonious and supportive dissertation committee. Thanks also to Boris Groysberg at Harvard Business School, who has given me the opportunity to do work that beautifully complements the Miss Conduct endeavor—and also time off to work on the book whenever I have requested it. A special thanks to Rivka Perlmann; I may have gotten the book done without you, but I sure as hell wouldn't have been able to enjoy it.

The special inner circle. Mom, you are the one who taught me that neither kindness nor intelligence is worth much without the other. Dad, you didn't live long enough to see my first book come out, but you never, ever doubted it would. Lance, you are my brother from another mother and I can't imagine life without you. Milo, you have brought to vivid life everything they tried to teach me in my psychology program. If I can cope gracefully with your values, priorities, and experiences, then surely nothing in the human world can seem all that alien to me. Marc, what is there to say? Our marriage is the house I live in. And this, as you often point out, is only the beginning.

Finally, thank you to my readers. "I'd be nothing without you" is metaphorical, however heartfelt. But when it comes to you, it's the God's honest. There ain't no advice columnist without questions. And your questions form the heart of this book. Thank you for sharing—your questions, your answers, your wit, your stories, your criticisms, your song parodies and fashion don'ts and clerihews.

There is so much in this book that I didn't write about. I didn't discuss addiction in the health and disability (or food) chapter. I barely touched on homosexuality and transsexuals in the sex and gender chapter. I didn't write about adopted children, or interracial families, or polyamory, or how to cope with a friend's (or your own) sudden unemployment. However thorough you try to be, the scope of the human experience will always outrun you. I chose to tackle the areas I get asked about most often . . . and hope, in the way of all authors, that this book's unanswered questions can be the basis of the next book. At the very least, I've tried to provide a framework for how to think about difference, even if I haven't hit on every possible form those differences can take.

Thank *you*, for reading all this way.

Index

About the Author

For Robin Abrahams, writing the weekly "Miss Conduct" column for the *Boston Globe Magazine* is the fulfillment of a lifetime dream—getting paid to tell people what to do. As a child she always identified with the character of Lucy in the *Peanuts* comic strip and was bitterly disappointed when her parents forced her to have a conventional lemonade stand rather than a booth for dispensing "psychiatric advice" at five cents per problem.

A research associate at Harvard Business School, Robin has also worked as a stand-up comedian, theater publicist, organizational-change communications manager, and professor of psychology. She earned her PhD in psychology from Boston University and has a BA in theater studies from the University of Kansas.

She is married to "Mr. Improbable," Marc Abrahams, the founder of the Ig Nobel Prizes, which are given annually for achievements that first make people laugh, and then make them think. Marc is also editor of the science humor magazine *Annals of Improbable Research* (www.improbable.com), for which Robin serves as psychology editor and writes an occasional column, "Socially Scientific." They live in Cambridge, Massachusetts, with their socially successful dog, Milo.

CPSIA information can be obtained
at www.ICGtesting.com
Printed in the USA
LVHW040322040423
743408LV00001B/75

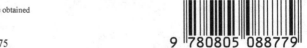